Mathematics, the Common Core, and RTI

This book is dedicated to my husband Bernard Burton, my hero, and the wind beneath my wings . . .

—Dolores Burton

. . . and to Catherine Faith Kappenberg . . . the love of my life and partner in everything I do.

—John Kappenberg

Mathematics, the Common Core, and RTI

An Integrated Approach to Teaching in Today's Classrooms

Dolores Burton

John Kappenberg

CORWIN
A SAGE Company

CORWIN
A SAGE Company

FOR INFORMATION:

Corwin
A SAGE Company
2455 Teller Road
Thousand Oaks, California 91320
(800) 233-9936
www.corwin.com

SAGE Publications Ltd.
1 Oliver's Yard
55 City Road
London EC1Y 1SP
United Kingdom

SAGE Publications India Pvt. Ltd.
B 1/I 1 Mohan Cooperative Industrial Area
Mathura Road, New Delhi 110 044
India

SAGE Publications Asia-Pacific Pte. Ltd.
3 Church Street
#10-04 Samsung Hub
Singapore 049483

Printed in the United States of America

Library of Congress Cataloging-in-Publication Data

Burton, Dolores.

Mathematics, the common core, and RTI : an integrated approach to teaching in today's classrooms / Dolores Burton, John Kappenberg.

pages cm
Includes bibliographical references and index.

ISBN 978-1-4522-5837-9 (pbk.)

1. Mathematics—Study and teaching—Standards—United States. 2. Response to intervention (Learning disabled children) I. Kappenberg, John. II. Title.

QA13.B868 2013
372.702′1873—dc23   2013020250

This book is printed on acid-free paper.

Acquisitions Editor: Jessica Allan
Associate Editor: Kimberly Greenberg
Editorial Assistant: Heidi Arndt
Production Editor: Melanie Birdsall
Copy Editor: Sarah J. Duffy
Typesetter: C&M Digitals (P) Ltd.
Proofreader: Victoria Reed-Castro
Indexer: Michael Ferreira
Cover Designer: Anupama Krishnan

13 14 15 16 17 10 9 8 7 6 5 4 3 2 1

Contents

Acknowledgments

I have been fortunate to know my mentor, former professor, and friend, Dr. Barbara Baskin, for 35 years. Without her encouragement so long ago, this book and many other accomplishments would not have been possible.

—*Dolores Burton*

I wish to thank my colleagues, past and present, for allowing me to be both a teacher and student throughout my career. For without those enriching and invaluable experiences, my contribution to this book and to education would not have been possible.

—*Harold J. Dean*

I am indebted to the teachers and leadership of Sandy Creek High School, in Sandy Creek, New York—Janice Burns, PPS coordinator; Kim Manfredi, special education teacher; and Jonna St. Croix, global studies teacher—for providing an outstanding example of an effective inclusion program. Their work served as a model for many of the observations and recommendations found in Chapter 7. Finally, I gratefully acknowledge almost 50 years of professional support and personal inspiration from Dick Maitland and more than 25 years of lessons in leadership, mentorship, and friendship from George Goldstein.

—*John Kappenberg*

Thank you to Barb Crandall, third-grade teacher and president-elect of the Alaska Council of Teachers of Mathematics, for her insightful comments. Special thanks to all of the staff at Corwin who supported us during completion of this book: Jessica Allan, senior acquisitions editor; Kimberly Greenberg, associate editor; Heidi Arndt, editorial assistant; Melanie Birdsall, production editor; Sarah J. Duffy, copy editor; Anupama Krishnan, cover designer; and Karen Ehrmann, permissions editor. And special thanks to Dr. Patricia Schmidt, Education Division Chair, Five Towns College, for reading the manuscript and sharing her scholarly perspectives.

—*Dolores Burton and John Kappenberg*

Publisher's Acknowledgments

Corwin gratefully acknowledges the contributions of the following reviewers:

Zoma Barrett
Math Teacher
Salem Middle School
Salem, IN

Deb Bible
RTI Interventionist
Dundee Highlands School
West Dundee, IL

Scott Currier
Math Teacher
Nute High School
Milton, NH

JoAnn Hiatt
Math Teacher
Olathe East High School
Olathe, KS

Judith A. Rogers
K–5 Mathematics Specialist
Tucson Unified School District
Tucson, AZ

Judith A. Ross
Educational Consultant/Teacher Liaison
Dartmouth College GK–12 Program
Hanover, NH

About the Authors

 **Dolores Burton, EdD,** is a Fulbright scholar, former public school teacher in middle and high school mathematics, and school district administrator implementing schoolwide, districtwide, and countywide educational technology programs including the design and supervision of infrastructure installation. She recently retired as professor and chair of teacher education at New York Institute of Technology. She has published in numerous journals, presented nationally and internationally, and consulted regionally, nationally, and internationally. Her numerous consultancies include service as a member of the New York State Education Department Panel of Experts Response to Intervention Policy Committee and lecturing on school reform strategies in Kenya.

Dr. Burton authored instructional software and is the co-author of *The Complete Guide to RTI: An Implementation Toolkit*. During her 37 years in education, she has designed, delivered, and supervised professional development for teachers in Grades K–12 in mathematics, literacy, science, differentiated instruction, action research, instructional technology, using data to drive instruction, and inclusive practices. She has organized symposia for educators and parents on research-based strategies to close the achievement gap of the traditionally underserved populations: African American males, English language learners, students with special needs, and others at risk for academic failure. Her research interests include Response to Intervention (RTI), teacher preparation (elementary through college), Common Core State Standards, professional development, using data to drive instruction, and using technology to teach all students, especially those who have traditionally been underserved.

 **John Kappenberg, EdD,** has spent 40 years in education as teacher, professor, district administrator, writer, speaker, and consultant to school districts and professional organizations. He is currently chair of medical education and program manager for the Accelerated D.O./Family Medicine Residency Continuum at the New York Institute of Technology (NYIT) College of Osteopathic Medicine. He was director of research, planning and quality at the Sewanhaka Central High School District in New York for 18 years, where he led its long-term Strategic Planning Program. He has been director of educational leadership and technology at NYIT and has taught school finance and law, Total Quality Management, strategic planning, teacher education, and educational technology at Hofstra University, Adelphi University, Touro College, St. Joseph's College on Long Island, and Argosy University in Sarasota, Florida. Dr. Kappenberg served on the Board of Directors for the New York State Governor's Excelsior Award Program, as audio and sound effects artist for ABC Television Network and *Sesame Street*, and has produced more than 120 instructional, motivational, and public information videos and DVDs for schools, universities, and professional and state organizations.

About the Contributors

Harold J. Dean, EdD, is an administrator with the Eastern Suffolk Board of Cooperative Education Services on Long Island. He has taught elementary and secondary special education across many settings, including inclusive, consultant, self-contained, and itinerant models. He has served as a central office administrator in managing a state personnel improvement grant focusing on improving special education practices through the use of best-practice partnerships. Currently, he is a building administrator at a career and technical education high school serving general education and classified populations. He has presented locally and nationally on topics including Response to Intervention; effective instructional practices and intervention models; collaborative partnerships; progress monitoring; and data-based decision making in curriculum, instruction, and assessment. Dr. Dean also teaches courses on leadership, professional development, collaboration, and reflective practice at the graduate level for St. Joseph's College School of Education in New York.

Helene Fallon, MEd, has a background in social work and education with extensive training in advocacy for children and young adults with disabilities. She is the parent of two children with special needs. Working nationally as a professional development specialist, she conducts trainings on many topics, always focusing on collaboration and effective communication in education.

Andrea Honigsfeld, EdD, is a professor in the Division of Education at Molloy College, in Rockville Centre, New York. She teaches graduate education courses related to cultural and linguistic diversity, linguistics, English as a second language (ESL) methodology, and action research. Before entering the field of teacher education, she taught English as a foreign language in Hungary, ESL in New York City, and Hungarian at New York University. She was the recipient of a doctoral fellowship at St. John's University, New York, where she conducted research on individualized instruction and learning styles. She has published extensively on working with English language learners and providing individualized instruction based on learning style preferences. She received a Fulbright Award to lecture in Iceland in the fall of 2002. She frequently offers staff development primarily focusing on effective differentiated strategies and collaborative practices for ESL and general education teachers. She co-authored *Collaboration and Co-Teaching: Strategies for English Learners* (2010, Corwin), *Common Core for the Not-So-Common Learner: K–5 English Language Arts Strategies* (2013, Corwin), *Common Core for the Not-So-Common Learner: 6–12 English Language Arts Strategies* (2013, Corwin), and co-edited *Coteaching and Other Collaborative Practices in the EFL/ESL Classroom: Rationale, Research, Reflections, and Recommendations* (2012) with Maria Dove. Her co-authored book *Differentiated Instruction for At-Risk Students* (2009) and co-edited five-volume Breaking the Mold of Education series (2010–2013) with Audrey Cohan were published by Rowman and Littlefield.

Charlotte Rosenzweig, EdD, is currently an adjunct professor of adolescent education in English language arts and literacy and supervisor of student teachers at Molloy College, in Rockville Centre, New York. She has also taught graduate and teacher education courses in curriculum and design, reading in the content areas 6–12, and remediation of reading problems at New York Institute of Technology, Center for Integrated Teacher Education, and Long Beach High School. As an educator and administrative leader in both urban and suburban settings for more than 30 years, Dr. Rosenzweig has served as an English chairperson, a curriculum associate (K–12), and an assistant principal and language arts coordinator. Prior to her administrative experiences, she served as a reading specialist and English language arts teacher. She presented for colleagues and peers at the Long Island Language Arts Council, American Education Research Association, Farmingdale Teacher Center, Hofstra University Doctoral Colloquium, Cold Spring Harbor Schools, and Nassau Reading Council. Dr. Rosenzweig received her doctorate from Hofstra University's Department of Foundations, Leadership and Policy Studies. Her publications include *A Meta-Analysis of Parenting and School Success: The Role of Parents in Promoting Students' Academic Performance* (2000), *PSAT/SAT Handbook* (2007), *A Journey Into Academe,* and the co-authored *The Path to Research* (2006).

1

Introduction to Mathematics, the Common Core, and RTI

The Common Core State Standards provide a consistent, clear under-standing of what students are expected to learn, so teachers and parents know what they need to do to help them. The standards are designed to be robust and relevant to the real world, reflecting the knowledge and skills that our young people need for success in college and careers. With American students fully prepared for the future, our communities will be best positioned to compete successfully in the global economy.

—Council of Chief State School Officers (2010, para. 1)

Today, most teachers, curriculum designers, and supervisors have a shelf full of books, articles, and reports introducing them to the requirements of the Common Core State Standards (CCSS) and the instructional framework known as Response to Intervention (RTI). One result of these multiple initiatives, regulations, and standards is a form of burnout known as "initiative fatigue" (Reeves, 2010). They would rather wait and hope that these complex initiatives will somehow go away, or at least not obstruct their teaching. At the same time, they know that the status quo in American schools is not acceptable. According to *Trends in International Mathematics and Science Study (TIMSS) 2011*, eight nations scored higher than the United States in fourth-grade mathematics and eleven countries scored higher in the eighth-grade level (Mullis, Martin, Foy, & Arora, 2012). Given the mediocre performance of American students on international assessments in mathematics, and the need to maintain a leadership position in the global economy, waiting for policy makers to produce a single, easy-to-implement plan is not an option.

Something has to be done in thousands of mathematics classes, in each individual school, by every teacher, using the programs in place now.

The most pervasive mandates in American schools today are the Common Core State Standards (prescribing the content of instruction) and Response to Intervention (prescribing a data-based method of instruction). Most of the resources available to help teachers work with either mandate treat the two as separate entities, without reference to the other. As a result, mathematics educators are calling for some way of working with CCSS and RTI as a single, unified program that they can use in their classes, rather than as separate, isolated mandates. Discussions with teachers reflect John F. Kennedy's frustration with his advisors when he reportedly complained, "All my economists say, 'on the one hand . . . on the other.' Give me a one-handed economist" (quoted in Krugman, 2003, p. 11). Teachers need a single integrated approach to mathematics instruction—not two, let alone three or more—that addresses the needs of all their students.

In preparation for this book, we reviewed the growing collection of material on CCSS and RTI that is available to educators, and as we listened to colleagues who are introducing the two programs to their schools, it became clear that what they needed was not another handbook telling them what CCSS or RTI is. What they want is, first, a way of untangling the perspectives of the many experts within the fields of the Common Core and RTI. Second, they are asking for help in charting a path through the potential interactions between RTI and the other mandated requirements their schools face, particularly the Common Core, but also the No Child Left Behind legislation, the National Council of Teachers of Mathematics Standards, differentiated instruction and universal design, inclusion, parent involvement, and the demands of their local school policies. Teaching mathematics is a more complex activity than ever before, and the need for a unified instructional strategy to teach all students has never been stronger. There is pressing need for a book that integrates the multiple new requirements into a single, comprehensible process that can help teachers succeed with the mandates of CCSS and RTI, but more important, to help each of their students achieve success in mathematics. That is our goal.

RTI and the Common Core: Casual Friends or the Dynamic Duo?

RTI and the Common Core both became national mandates as part of the shift in educational values launched by the No Child Left Behind Act of 2001: clear and consistent standards (the Common Core), universal screening and response to the needs of struggling students (RTI), and greater accountability for success in every aspect of public education. Taken individually, RTI and the Common Core each produced a shift of paradigms as we moved from 20th to 21st century education. Each of them presents a formidable task for teachers. Together, they create a perfect storm of challenges. Teachers need to untangle their multiple demands and find a way to transform the two mandates into a single unified process within a school's mathematics program. This calls for placing RTI and the Common Core into a new integrated perspective and in context with the complex world that educators face every day.

Mathematics, the Common Core, and RTI: An Integrated Approach to Teaching in Today's Classrooms addresses this need by developing an integrated approach for introducing RTI and the Common Core to professional educators and to teacher candidates in colleges and universities. The chapters to guide that path are outlined below.

Chapter 2, "Marching Together to Academic Success," reviews the history and importance of the Common Core State Standards for Mathematics (including the Standards for Mathematical Practice and Standards for Mathematical Content) and their relation to RTI. It then expands on a practical approach to Response to Intervention, as presented in our previous work, *The Complete Guide to RTI: An Implementation Toolkit* (Burton & Kappenberg, 2012). Finally, it presents an approach for integrating the academic content and standards of the Common Core for Mathematics with the diagnostic and instructional framework of RTI. The remaining chapters apply this framework to several of the key elements of mathematics instruction, including strategies for students who struggle with mathematics.

Chapter 3, "Universal Design and Mathematics: A Framework for RTI and Implementing the Common Core," describes how an understanding of the principles of universal design can help teachers meet the diverse needs of their students. It presents practical approaches that can help teachers seamlessly integrate the knowledge base of current brain-based research into the principles of universal design that has become essential to school programs in recent years. The chapter begins with a presentation of recent brain-based research behind Universal Design for Learning (UDL). It reviews the three commonly identified neural networks of the brain that are central to the UDL process:

1. *Recognition networks:* the area in the brain that processes the contents—the what—of learning

2. *Strategic networks:* the area in the brain that processes the method—the how—of learning

3. *Affective networks:* the area in the brain that processes the meaning—the why—of learning

The discussion includes a summary of the nine principles of UDL:

1. *Equitable use*, which ensures the design is useful to people with diverse abilities

2. *Flexibility in use*, which assures that instruction provides opportunities for choice of instructional media and methods

3. *Simple and intuitive use*, which focuses on the need to eliminate unnecessary complexity in instructions for mathematics assignments

4. *Perceptible information*, which addresses the need for appropriate methods of communicating information, regardless of the student's sensory abilities

5. *Tolerance for error*, which minimizes mathematical errors by assessing students' current level of competence and prerequisite skills

6. *Low physical effort*, which emphasizes the design of mathematics instruction so that students quickly recognize errors and minimize their repetition

7. *Size and space for approach and use*, which reminds us to design instructional settings that provide a clear line of sight to all important instructional elements, such as the blackboard

8. *Creating a community of learners*, which promotes interaction and communication among students and provides opportunities for collaborative problem solving

9. *Creating a welcoming and inclusive environment*, which includes holding high expectations for all students and a policy of zero tolerance for negativity

Several specific examples are provided, demonstrating how to use the principles of UDL to improve the performance of students who struggle in mathematics in the Common Core content and the RTI instructional framework. Chapter 3 concludes with examples of mathematics lessons appropriate for Tiers 1, 2, and 3.

Chapter 4, "Progress Monitoring: Avoiding a Blind Date With Data," begins with a definition of progress monitoring (PM). The chapter reviews the research evidence supporting the effectiveness of PM in diagnosing how well students are prepared for academic work, how it can guide instructional decisions, and its role in the RTI framework. The review focuses specifically on the use of PM in measuring student growth and outcomes according to the Common Core State Standards in mathematics. The chapter is framed around the six basic stages of progress monitoring:

1. Define the behavior: What do my students need to learn?

2. Select the measurement strategy: How do I know my students are learning?

3. Establish baseline assessment scores: Where are my students presently?

4. Create a goal: Where do my students need to be?

5. Develop a chart or graph: Are my students growing?

6. Create a decision-making plan: How do I get my students to where they need to be?

Chapter 4 concludes with a discussion of why it is important for teachers to use progress monitoring as a data gathering and analysis tool within the RTI framework to fully implement the Common Core State Standards.

Chapter 5, "Connecting Mathematics and Literacy: If a Picture Is Worth a Thousand Words, How Many Words Is an Equation Worth?" develops the idea that, from the earliest years of instruction, mathematics needs to be presented as a language in its own right and also one that uses English as part of its own special vocabulary. The chapter begins with a definition of mathematics literacy and describes seven strategies for promoting it, along with activities to develop mathematics literacy in class. The chapter then focuses on specific provisions of the Common Core State Standards that address math literacy and offers ideas on connecting these standards to the screening processes used in a Response to Intervention program. This leads to an extended review of seven strategies for integrating literacy into instruction in mathematics guided by the Common Core:

- Strategy 1: Authentic performance tasks
- Strategy 2: Cooperative learning, metacognition, and verbal discourse in mathematics instruction
- Strategy 3: Teaching vocabulary using five types of context clues
- Strategy 4: Use of graphic organizers
- Strategy 5: Games, magic squares, and puzzles
- Strategy 6: Oral reading of children's books
- Strategy 7: Direct instruction in mathematics vocabulary

Chapter 5 concludes with specific examples of ways to introduce math literacy activities into each of the three tiers of a school's RTI program.

Chapter 6, "English Language Learners," shows how the approaches to mathematics instruction outlined in Chapter 3 (UDL) and Chapter 5 (math literacy) can be applied to English language learners (ELLs). Here again, the complex demands of the Common Core in mathematics and Response to

Intervention need to be untangled so that teachers can develop a focused and coherent approach as they introduce these programs to their instruction. Chapter 6 provides guidelines to help accomplish this. It begins with a review of the most critical barrier that ELLs typically face: the error that teachers and schools frequently make in mistaking mathematics difficulty for mathematics disability. While only 6%–7% of the general population is known to have a clinical disability in learning mathematics (Fuchs & Fuchs, 2005), a much higher percentage of ELLs receive this classification in our schools (Flores, Batalova, & Fix, 2012). Chapter 6 examines the reasons for the discrepancy. It then discusses the difference for ELLs between their acquisition of social language and the academic language they need to succeed in mathematics. It presents strategies for teaching the Common Core content in mathematics to ELLs in each of the three tiers of RTI. The chapter concludes with examples of differences in mathematics teaching and learning between various cultures and examples of CCSS-aligned lessons in Tiers 1, 2, and 3.

Chapter 7, "Teaching Mathematics in an Inclusion Classroom Guided by the Common Core," extends the applications of RTI and the Common Core to a challenge that now faces almost every mathematics teacher: the inclusion setting. Inclusion can take a wide range of forms, but in most cases it calls for a special education teacher (who may have little expertise in mathematics) to work with a certified mathematics teacher (who usually has little knowledge of the learning needs of students with disabilities and other learning challenges). The task of inclusion is to combine their expertise and design a new approach to instruction that meets the needs of both the general education and special needs students in the same classroom, using the same curriculum content. Not since the K–12 one-room schoolhouse of a century ago have teachers been required to be so adaptive and creative.

In one sense, inclusion—the mandate that most special needs students be educated in the same classes, using the same curriculum, as their general education peers—is the ultimate standard for both the RTI framework and the Common Core content.

The chapter explains the hierarchy of relationships among the Common Core, RTI, and inclusion that can be used to design a unified educational program for an inclusion class. The key to success is the level of preparation for both the professional staff and the students. The kinds of preparation needed are discussed in detail.

Chapter 7 presents practical ideas on teaching the Common Core mathematics curriculum within an RTI framework in an inclusion setting. The interrelationship among these is emphasized and reference is made to the practical legal requirements that schools need to follow to protect the rights of all students—both special education and general education—in an inclusion class.

One of the central strategies for inclusion is the variety of co-teaching models available to professionals. These are analyzed with an eye toward helping teachers understand which strategies are most likely to be successful in their own setting, and also when several different approaches may be needed within the same classroom. Chapter 7 then discusses another important aspect of co-teaching: the shared and complementary roles of the general education mathematics teacher and the special education teacher. Critical elements of co-teaching, such as common planning time, are emphasized.

Chapter 7 continues with examples of mathematics lessons that can be taught in inclusion settings for Tier 1 and Tier 2. It concludes with a discussion of the wide range of groups in addition to "classic" special education students, that need to be recognized in designing an inclusion program in mathematics: talented and gifted, twice exceptional (special needs students who are also talented and gifted), ESL students, and others.

Chapter 8, "The Role of Parents Helping Students to Achieve," introduces a professional skill that is rarely covered systematically in teacher preparation and is often lacking, even in veteran teachers: the strategies needed to develop a productive relationship between teachers and parents. This is particularly critical in programs based on RTI and the Common Core, which place new emphasis on the needs of individual students. As educational practice becomes more focused on the individual student—in conjunction with group instruction—the need for parental involvement, support, and consultation has increased significantly. This chapter presents approaches that can lead to parent involvement that enhances, rather than obstructs, math instruction.

Chapter 8 introduces contrasting approaches to the teacher-parent relationship: the traditional "client relationship" and an alternative "consultant relationship." The client relationship assumes that the teacher possesses the professional training to make decisions about a student's educational program, and the parent's role is to support these decisions. The consultant relationship recognizes the professional judgment of the teacher but adds to this the teacher's need for insights into the student that only the parent can provide. The parent is seen as an essential resource in designing the individual program for the student, which is particularly critical in approaches to instruction that are based on the Common Core, RTI, and Universal Design for Learning.

We then use role-playing scenarios of teacher-parent conversations to illustrate how these approaches differ, what they sound like in practice, and the contrasting outcomes of each. Chapter 8 concludes with an extensive list of resources for facilitating the collaboration process between parents and teachers, and online resources devoted to RTI and the Common Core that are available to parents and educators.

Before we can forge that path, we need to enhance our knowledge base of the Common Core and RTI. Chapter 2 is designed to do just that. The adventure has begun!

2 Marching Together to Academic Success

Implementation of the standards is now the key challenge. Properly done, the standards will gain traction and the students will gain knowledge and skills. This is a huge undertaking for the United States, but what could be more important?

—Chester E. Finn Jr., President, Thomas B. Fordham Institute

In this chapter you will learn:

- What are the Common Core State Standards?
- How can we design lesson plans to reflect the new expectations of the Common Core?
- How are the Standards for Mathematical Practice connected to the Standards for Mathematical Content?
- How do the CCSS relate to Response to Intervention?
- How do we implement the Common Core State Standards for mathematics into the classroom in an RTI framework?

The Common Core State Standards (CCSS)

In today's global economy, where events halfway around the world can instantaneously impact our present and future, we must prepare our students to compete with the intellectual and problem-solving skills they will need, particularly in the emerging STEM fields of science, technology, engineering, and mathematics. Over the past decade, renowned experts have collaborated in efforts such as the Mathematics Learning Study Committee

(Kilpatrick, Swafford, & Findell, 2001) and the National Mathematics Advisory Panel (2008) to address the task of increasing mathematics proficiency in our students.

To create clear academic benchmarks to reach that goal, in September 2009 the National Governor's Association (NGA) and Council of Chief State School Officers (CCSSO) published the college and career-ready standards (Grossman, Reyna, & Shipto, 2011). In December 2009 the first draft of the Common Core was published. It was released to the public for comment in March 2010 and finalized in the publication released on June 2, 2010 (CCSSO, 2010).

The standards they developed are research and evidence based and internationally benchmarked. As of January 2013, they had been adopted by nearly every state (with the exception of Alaska, Nebraska, Minnesota, Virginia, and Texas) and the American Samoa Islands, Guam, the Northern Mariana Islands, the U.S. Virgin Islands, and the District of Columbia. The focus of the standards is to

- provide clarity about the specific academic content that students are expected to learn in mathematics and English language arts,
- help teachers zero in on the most important knowledge and skills they need to teach, and
- help states and districts assess the effectiveness of educational programs and instructional methods.

Common learning goals within the CCSS for mathematics were intended to provide a clear vision for educators, students, and parents in all states and to help ensure that students meet college and work expectations and are prepared to succeed in a global economy. They are also an attempt to systematically align common K–12 mathematics standards across the states.

The foundation of the Standards is built on previous efforts, including the National Council of Teachers of Mathematics (NCTM) standards documents (1989, 2000; Schielack et al., 2006), but is a significant departure in several critical areas. The Common Core State Standards document describes it this way:

> These Standards are not intended to be new names for old ways of doing business. They are a call to take the next step. It is time for states to work together to build on lessons learned from two decades of standards based reforms. It is time to recognize that standards are not just promises to our children, but promises we intend to keep (CCSSO, 2010, p. 5).

The Common Core State Standards are different in scope and in required depth of understanding from past national and state standards at each grade level. The scope of the standards is narrow and deep, rather than broad and less intense, and there are significant changes in the approach to the content, in the placement of content by grade level, and in curriculum emphasis.

CCSS is based on an overriding vision: to be successful in mathematics and in life, our students need to have a conceptual understanding in mathematics, the skills to carry out procedures accurately and appropriately and to solve mathematical problems. Just as important, perhaps more important, is the disposition to see mathematics as useful and important to their futures. CCSS documents can help teachers design their instruction so students can develop both the essential mathematical skills and habits of mind needed to understand why these skills are important to their personal lives.

The standards are organized as *Standards for Mathematical Practice* and *Standards for Mathematical Content*. The Standards for Mathematical Practices focus on the varieties of mathematical expertise and thinking (processes and proficiencies), which educators at all levels believe will benefit their students in college and careers. These are defined as the "varieties of mathematical expertise and thinking that educators at all levels should seek to develop in their students" (CCSSO, 2010, p. 6), and include the following:

1. Make sense of problems and persevere in solving them.

2. Reason abstractly and quantitatively.

3. Construct viable arguments and critique the reasoning of others.

4. Model with mathematics.

5. Use appropriate tools strategically.

6. Attend to precision.

7. Look for and make use of structure.

8. Look for and express regularity in repeated reasoning.

Standards for Mathematical Content refer to the important understandings and deep conceptual knowledge necessary to succeed in college and careers. Let's first take a look at the Standards for Mathematical Practice.

STANDARDS FOR MATHEMATICAL PRACTICE

Standards for Mathematical Practice rest on the eight important processes and proficiencies within mathematics education. The first five are based on the NCTM process standards of problem solving, reasoning and proof, communication, representation, and connections. The second group, six through eight, is based on the strands of mathematical proficiency specified in the National Research Council's report *Adding It Up* (Kilpatrick et al., 2001).

The Standards for Mathematical Practice document the habits of mind that students need to develop. The practices provide a detailed description of the *way* mathematics should be learned and used. Teachers should try to include all eight of the Standards for Mathematical Practice in every unit of instruction, although all eight will not necessarily be featured in every lesson within the unit. These practices are the foundation of the effective application of mathematical content. The eight practices build on the process standards from NCTM (2000) and the strands of mathematical proficiency (Kilpatrick et al., 2001). They describe what it means to really "do" mathematics. Table 2.1 describes the practices and what they look like in a sixth-grade mathematics lesson.

Explicit instruction in mathematical practices may be helpful to students. For example, helping students use charts to solve problems can provide a structure for students to state what is known about a problem and what needs to be determined (Practice 4). Using mathematics journals to document the steps a student is taking to solve a problem and identifying the reasons for each step can address Practice 3. These practices can be used with students from kindergarten or first grade through eighth grade or in some cases in high school.

Educators also need to

- develop students' conceptual understanding of key mathematical concepts,
- set an expectation of fluency, and
- design applications (activities) that engage the students' interest without becoming a distraction from the content that needs to be learned.

To help teachers maintain focus and rigor, the Common Core State Standards are organized according to priorities for each grade level. We will be returning to these later in this chapter.

STANDARDS FOR MATHEMATICAL CONTENT

The Standards for Mathematical Content are "a balanced combination of procedure and understanding" (CCSSO, 2010, p. 8) for mathematics instruction within the Common Core. They are presented by grade level in Grades K–8 and are organized into standards that define what students

Table 2.1   Unpacking the Standards for Mathematical Practice

Standards for Mathematical Practice	Examples of How the Practices May Be Integrated Into Grade 6 Tasks
1. Make sense of problems and persevere in solving them.	Students solve real-world problems through the application of algebraic and geometric concepts. These problems involve ratio, rate, area, and statistics. Students seek the meaning of a problem and look for efficient ways to represent and solve it. They may check their thinking by asking themselves: What is the most efficient way to solve the problem? Does this make sense? Can I solve the problem in a different way? Students can explain the relationships between equations, verbal descriptions, tables, and graphs. Mathematically proficient students check answers to problems using a different method.
2. Reason abstractly and quantitatively.	Students represent a wide variety of real-world contexts in mathematical expressions, equations, and inequalities through the use of real numbers and variables. Students contextualize to understand the meaning of the number or variable as related to the problem and decontextualize to manipulate symbolic representations by applying properties of operations.
3. Construct viable arguments and critique the reasoning of others.	Students construct arguments using verbal or written explanations accompanied by expressions, equations, inequalities, models and graphs, tables, and other data displays (e.g., box plots, dot plots, histograms). They further refine their mathematical communication skills through mathematical discussions in which they critically evaluate their own thinking and the thinking of other students. They pose questions (e.g., How did you get that? Why is that true? Does that always work?). They explain their thinking to others and respond to others' thinking.
4. Model with mathematics.	Students model problem situations symbolically, graphically, tabularly, and contextually. Students form expressions, equations, or inequalities from real-world contexts and connect symbolic and graphical representations. Students begin to explore covariance and represent two quantities simultaneously. Students use number lines to compare numbers and represent inequalities. They use measures of center and variability and data displays (e.g., box plots, histograms) to draw inferences about and make comparisons between data sets. Students need many opportunities to connect and explain the connections between the different representations. They should be able to use all of these representations as appropriate to a problem context.

Standards for Mathematical Practice	*Examples of How the Practices May Be Integrated Into Grade 6 Tasks*
5. Use appropriate tools strategically.	Students consider available tools (including estimation and technology) when solving a mathematical problem and decide when certain tools might be helpful. For instance, students in Grade 6 may decide to represent figures on the coordinate plane to calculate area. Number lines are used to understand division and to create dot plots, histograms, and box plots to visually compare the center and variability of the data. Additionally, students might use physical objects or applets to construct nets and calculate the surface area of three-dimensional figures.
6. Attend to precision.	Students continue to refine their mathematical communication skills by using clear and precise language in their discussions with others and in their own reasoning. Students use appropriate terminology when referring to rates, ratios, geometric figures, data displays, and components of expressions, equations, or inequalities.
7. Look for and make use of structure.	Students routinely seek patterns or structures to model and solve problems. For instance, students recognize patterns that exist in ratio tables, recognizing both the additive and multiplicative properties. Students apply properties to generate equivalent expressions (e.g., $6 + 2x = 3(2 + x)$ by distributive property) and solve equations (e.g., $2c + 3 = 15$, $2c = 12$) by subtraction property of equality ($c = 6$ by division property of equality). Students compose and decompose two- and three-dimensional figures to solve real-world problems involving area and volume.
8. Look for and express regularity in repeated reasoning.	Students use repeated reasoning to understand algorithms and make generalizations about patterns. During multiple opportunities to solve and model problems, they may notice that $a/b \div c/d = ad/bc$ and construct other examples and models that confirm their generalization. Students connect place value and their prior work with operations to understand algorithms to fluently divide multi-digit numbers and perform all operations with multi-digit decimals. Students informally begin to make connections between covariance, rates, and representations showing the relationships between quantities.

Source: North Carolina Department of Public Instruction (2012).

The stress on a "balanced combination of procedure and understanding" means that, in a Common Core framework, the most critical aspect of instruction is a continual reference to students' *understanding* of mathematics—as evidenced by their ability to *explain* how and why they followed a particular strategy in solving a mathematical problem.

should understand and be able to do; clusters, groups of related standards; and domains, larger groups of related standards that may progress over several grades.

The Common Core document provides introductions by grade and gives two to four focal points at each grade level. For high school–level content, the standards are presented by conceptual theme (Number & Quantity, Algebra, Functions, Modeling, Geometry, Statistics & Probability).

The content standards set priorities for broad topics by grade level. The narrative describes the organization of standards, within a cluster and within a domain. Figure 2.1 illustrates these components as presented in the *New York State P–12 Common Core Learning Standards for Mathematics* (New York State Education Department, 2012).

The stress on a "balanced combination of procedure and understanding" means that, in a Common Core framework, the most critical aspect of instruction is a continual reference to students' *understanding* of mathematics—as evidenced by their ability to *explain* how and why they followed a particular strategy in solving a mathematical problem. Without this level of understanding, students will never be able to make use of any skill or process to solve problems in the real world or in the future.

Figure 2.1   How to Read the Common Core State Standards Document

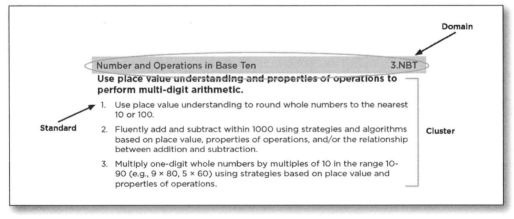

Figure 2.2 describes the CCSS priorities that support rich instruction for Grades K–8 in mathematics, as defined by the New York State Education Department and displayed on the website www.engageny.org.

Now that we have reviewed an example of the instructional priorities for a particular grade level, we can look at more detailed topics that the CCSS recommend as a focus for each grade. The topics from the Common Core document for kindergarten through eighth grade are found in Table 2.2.

Connecting the Standards for Mathematical Practice to the Standards for Mathematical Content

The Standards for Mathematical Practice describe ways in which students can grow and engage with mathematics. To accomplish this, the Standards for Mathematical Content present a balanced combination of procedure and

Figure 2.2   Priorities in Mathematics Instruction Guided by the Common Core State Standards by Grade Level for Grades K–8

Priorities in Math

Grade	Priorities in Support of Rich Instruction and Expectations of Fluency and Conceptual Understanding
K–2	Addition and subtraction, measurement using whole number quantities
3–5	Multiplication and division of whole numbers and fractions
6	Ratios and proportional reasoning; early expressions and equations
7	Ratios and proportional reasoning; arithmetic of rational numbers
8	Linear algebra

www.engageNY.org   112

Table 2.2   Recommended Common Core State Standards Topics for the Focus of Instructional Time and Resources by Grade Level

Grade Level	Focus of Instructional Time and Resources
Kindergarten	Instructional time should focus on two critical areas: (1) representing and comparing whole numbers, initially with sets of objects; (2) describing shapes and space.
Grade 1	Instructional time should focus on four critical areas: (1) developing understanding of addition, subtraction, and strategies for addition and subtraction within 20; (2) developing understanding of whole number relationships and place value, including grouping in tens and ones; (3) developing understanding of linear measurement and measuring lengths as iterating length units; and (4) reasoning about attributes of and composing and decomposing geometric shapes.
Grade 2	Instructional time should focus on four critical areas: (1) extending understanding of base-10 notation; (2) building fluency with addition and subtraction; (3) using standard units of measure; and (4) describing and analyzing shapes.
Grade 3	Instructional time should focus on four critical areas: (1) developing understanding of multiplication and division and strategies for multiplication and division within 100; (2) developing understanding of fractions, especially unit fractions (fractions with numerator 1); (3) developing understanding of the structure of rectangular arrays and of area; and (4) describing and analyzing two-dimensional shapes.
Grade 4	Instructional time should focus on three critical areas: (1) developing understanding and fluency with multi-digit multiplication, and developing understanding of dividing to find quotients involving multi-digit dividends; (2) developing an understanding of fraction equivalence, addition and subtraction of fractions with like denominators, and multiplication of fractions by whole numbers; (3) understanding that geometric figures can be analyzed and classified based on their properties, such as having parallel sides, perpendicular sides, particular angle measures, and symmetry.
Grade 5	Instructional time should focus on three critical areas: (1) developing fluency with addition and subtraction of fractions, and developing understanding of the multiplication of fractions and of division of fractions in limited cases (unit fractions divided by whole numbers and whole numbers divided by unit fractions); (2) extending division to two-digit divisors, integrating decimal fractions into the place value system, developing understanding of operations with decimals to hundredths, and developing fluency with whole number and decimal operations; and (3) developing understanding of volume.

Grade Level	Focus of Instructional Time and Resources
Grade 6	Instructional time should focus on four critical areas: (1) connecting ratio and rate to whole number multiplication and division and using concepts of ratio and rate to solve problems; (2) completing understanding of division of fractions and extending the notion of number to the system of rational numbers, which includes negative numbers; (3) writing, interpreting, and using expressions and equations; and (4) developing understanding of statistical thinking.
Grade 7	Instructional time should focus on four critical areas: (1) developing understanding of and applying proportional relationships; (2) developing understanding of operations with rational numbers and working with expressions and linear equations; (3) solving problems involving scale drawings and informal geometric constructions, and working with two- and three-dimensional shapes to solve problems involving area, surface area, and volume; and (4) drawing inferences about populations based on samples.
Grade 8	Instructional time should focus on three critical areas: (1) formulating and reasoning about expressions and equations, including modeling an association in bivariate data with a linear equation, and solving linear equations and systems of linear equations; (2) grasping the concept of a function and using functions to describe quantitative relationships; (3) analyzing two- and three-dimensional space and figures using distance, angle, similarity, and congruence, and understanding and applying the Pythagorean Theorem.

Source: © Copyright 2010. National Governors Association Center for Best Practices and Council of Chief State School Officers. All rights reserved.

conceptual understanding. This balance is critical because, as we know, when students do not have a clear understanding of a topic in mathematics, they tend to revert to a mechanical reliance on procedures alone. This leaves them unable to confront, or even understand, real-world problems. Without a clear understanding of mathematical processes, they are less likely to comprehend complex problems, use mathematics to design practical situations, have the skills to explain mathematics accurately to other students, or deviate from a known procedure to find an answer, even if it is the best choice for the particular problem. In short, a lack of deep understanding of concepts prevents students from using mathematics outside the classroom, in the real world, which is the ultimate goal of teaching mathematics in school.

The content standards set benchmarks of student understanding that are needed to link the Standards for Mathematical Content and the Standards for Mathematical Practice within an instructional program.

Common Core State Standards and
Response to Intervention: The Dynamic Duo

WHAT IS RTI?

Response to Intervention (RTI) is a multi-tiered framework designed to help struggling learners by systematically evaluating their academic performance and indicating the need for alternative interventions when current approaches are not successful. The performance and progress of each student is closely monitored (a process known as *progress monitoring*; see Chapter 4) to assess both the rate of learning and level of performance. Monitoring begins at the earliest stage of instruction and continues regularly throughout the year. When these assessments indicate that a student is struggling, alternative approaches to instruction (known as *interventions*) are introduced. Educational decisions about the intensity and duration of intervention are based on individual student response to instruction. Most RTI models include a three-tier, or three-step, process of increasing levels of support for students that includes high-quality classroom and screening interventions in general educational class settings (Tier 1), targeted small-group intervention (Tier 2), intensive interventions in addition to core instruction and comprehensive evaluation (Tier 3), or referral to evaluation for special education (Buffum, Mattos, & Weber, 2010). RTI requires high-quality, differentiated instruction for all students and also the close involvement of parents as a resource in understanding the unique needs of each student (RTI Action Network, n.d., para. 1).

> The principles of focus and coherence in CCSS support RTI by giving clear guidance on the benchmark mathematical concepts that we want students to understand and operations we want students to be able to do at each grade level.

Most important, in each tier teachers should be continually differentiating their instruction, based on insights into students' mathematical thinking as well as their academic performance. RTI is about knowing where each student is and keeping track of his or her progress (and thinking). The principles of focus and coherence in CCSS support RTI by giving clear guidance on the benchmark mathematical concepts that we want students to understand and operations we want students to be able to do at each grade level.

We can think of the three tiers of RTI as divided into two spheres: academic and behavioral. As Figure 2.3 suggests, these spheres reflect and reinforce one another and are essentially inseparable.

The model is based on the clinical understanding that all human behavior, including academic performance and social interaction, is rooted in a single complex dynamic, and that teachers should not view either the academic or the social behavior of their students in isolation. This insight is

Figure 2.3   The Spheres of Response to Intervention

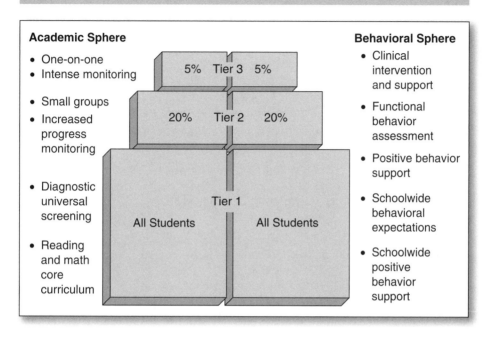

critically important in designing interventions and evaluating their effect in an RTI framework. It also points to the importance of including the insights of parents in working with individual students (see Chapter 8).

In the academic sphere of Tier 1, all students are given universal diagnostic screening and a research-based curriculum delivered with effective teaching strategies. The behavioral sphere includes schoolwide behavioral expectations and general behavioral support. For the approximately 20% of students who do not succeed with the classwide academic and/or behavioral supports of Tier 1, Tier 2 provides more intensive instruction in small groups with more frequent progress monitoring in the academic sphere and functional behavioral assessment and positive behavioral supports in the behavioral sphere. For the approximately 5% of students who do not succeed in Tier 2, the Tier 3 academic sphere provides intensive one-on-one instruction and increased monitoring, while the behavioral sphere may introduce clinical intervention by a qualified professional, such as a social worker, psychologist, or behavioral analyst. Note that these are general guidelines for an RTI model and that the actual services provided in a particular situation will depend entirely on the needs of individual students and the resources available in the school.

In this book we will focus on the academic sphere as it applies to the subject of mathematics. More information regarding the behavioral sphere can be found in an earlier work, *The Complete Guide to Response to Intervention: An Implementation Toolkit* (Burton & Kappenberg, 2012).

A Moment to Discuss Effective Instructional Strategies

In all three tiers, students should receive instruction based on research-supported best practices. Gerstan and Clarke (2007) have identified some instructional strategies for helping students with difficulties in mathematics:

- Structured peer-assisted learning activities
- Systematic and explicit instruction using visual representations
- Modifying instruction based on data from formative assessments (such as classroom discussions or quizzes)
- Providing opportunities for students to think aloud while they work

Mathematics instruction should emphasize three key ideas:

Focus: Emphasize areas on which the standards focus. Narrow the number of topics in each grade so that students more deeply experience the subjects that remain.

Coherence: Make connections across grades, and link major topics within grades. The most important connections are vertical, linking one grade to the next.

Rigor: Pursue conceptual understanding, procedural skill and fluency, and applications with equal intensity. (New York State Education Department, 2012)

Tier 1 Mathematics Instruction: Meeting the Needs of All Students Guided by the CCSS

After familiarizing you with the topics from the recommended Common Core State Standards, the next section of this chapter will illustrate how to develop lesson plans aligned with the CCSS for mathematics that can address the needs of individual students as well as an entire class. We will use a sample lesson addressing the seventh-grade Common Core State Standard on probability. The lesson plan is created using a template that will be available to readers as a black line master for any lesson plan addressing a common core standard. Always remember that, in a CCSS framework, we start with a standard, such as those illustrated in Figure 2.1. These provide the essential direction and goal for each classroom academic activity.

Let's take a look at the seventh-grade lesson plan in Table 2.3.

A lesson plan template follows that can be used or adapted for your CCSS guided lessons. Please feel free to copy or adapt the template in Table 2.4 as you unpack the CCSS in your instruction in the RTI framework.

Table 2.3   Lesson Plan: Introduction to Probability of Independent and Compound Events

Class	Seventh-grade mathematics
Tier	1
Standard(s)	**7.SP.C.5:** Understand that the probability of a chance event is a number between 0 and 1 that expresses the likelihood of the event occurring. Larger numbers indicate greater likelihood. A probability near 0 indicates an unlikely event, a probability around 1/2 indicates an event that is neither unlikely nor likely, and a probability near 1 indicates a likely event.
Guiding Questions	**Essential Question:** How can I use probability to make wise decisions in my life? Ask students to write questions in their mathematics journal. • What is probability? • How do we determine probability? • How do we use probability in real-life situations?
Student-Friendly Objectives	Students will determine the likelihood, or probability, of an event. Using hands-on inquiry, students will discover the rule for finding the probability of a single event and two independent events. Students will understand the relationship between probability and the likelihood of an event occurring.
Academic Vocabulary	*Probability* is the precise measure of how likely it is that an event will happen. An *experiment* is a situation involving chance or probability that leads to results called *outcomes* (Mrs. Glosser's Math Goodies, 1998–2013). An *outcome* is the result of a single trial of an experiment. An *event* is one or more outcomes of an experiment. A *compound event* is an event that consists of two or more events that are not mutually exclusive. Two events, A and B, are *independent* if the fact that A occurs does not affect the probability of B occurring.
Student Engagement	In this lesson, students use a hands-on approach to explore the probability of choosing a particular color pair of socks. Each student has an active role in the inquiry process.

(Continued)

Table 2.3   (Continued)

Mini Lesson	1. Show lottery tickets and discuss the odds of winning. What decision would you make based on this information? Create several examples of the use of probability in real life and ask students to think about how probability can help them make good decisions.
	2. Divide the class into groups of four. Review the vocabulary, then demonstrate an example of an event by having students pick a marble from a clear glass bowl containing five different color marbles and demonstrate how to calculate the probability of drawing a specific color marble. Then tell a story about the electricity going out and needing to take a pair of socks out of a drawer to wear with your green dress (or pants) without being able to see what color the socks are. Then say, "The dresser drawer contains one pair of socks with each of the following colors: blue, brown, red, white, and black. Each pair is folded together in a matching set. You reach into the sock drawer and choose a pair of socks without looking. You replace this pair and then choose another pair of socks. What is the probability of getting a pair of green socks?"
	3. Give each group of students a cardboard box representing a dresser draw with blue, green, red, white, and black paper "socks." Each pair is paper clipped together in a matching set. Have students reach into the sock drawer and choose a pair of socks without looking. Have them replace this pair and then choose another pair of socks. Then ask, "What is the probability that you will choose the red pair of socks both times?"
	4. A jar contains 1 red, 1 green, 1 purple, 1 blue, and 1 yellow marble. A marble is chosen at random from the jar. After replacing it, a second marble is chosen. What is the probability (P) of choosing a green and then a yellow marble? $$P \text{ (green)} = 1/5 \qquad P \text{ (yellow)} = 1/5$$ $$P \text{ (green and yellow)} = P \text{ (green)} \times P \text{ (yellow)}$$ $$1/5 \times 1/5 = 1/25 \qquad 1/25 = .04$$ The probability of choosing a green marble and a yellow marble is 1/25, or .04.
	5. Demonstrate one more example: The probability of landing on heads after tossing a coin *and* rolling a 5 on a single 6-sided die.
	6. Review the lesson up to this point by asking students to create the rule for finding the probability of two independent events: When two events, A and B, are independent, the probability of both occurring is: $P(A \text{ and } B) = P(A) \times P(B)$ (Multiplication Rule)

	7. Reinforce the concept of independent events by closing the teacher talk part of the lesson with a review: "Choosing a pair of socks from the drawer, replacing it, and then choosing a pair again from the same drawer is a compound event. Since the first pair is replaced, choosing a red pair on the first try has no effect on the probability of choosing a red pair on the second try. Therefore, these events are independent."
	8. Summarize the lesson for the students.
Differentiate	*English language learners.* Preteach vocabulary to English language learners or other students that may struggle with reading academic language. Some students may need reinforcement or preteaching using media. Videos on probability can be found at www.khanacademy.org/math/trigonometry/prob_comb/basic_prob_precalc/v/basic-probability.
Performance Task	Each student is given a different task in the group based on preferences and ability: a scribe to record the outcomes of the sock experiment using the mathematics vocabulary for the lesson, a "sock picker" to reach into the box with eyes closed to pick a pair of socks, a facilitator to lead the group discussion as they calculate the probability of picking each color after 10 events (the sock is replaced after each event), and the reporter that reports out to the class at the end of the experiment on how the group arrived at the answer.
Assessment	Have students flip a coin 20 times independently and calculate the probability of landing on heads. Have students write in their math journal the process they followed and the answer to the problem.
Technology Resources	See www.sharemylesson.com/teaching-resource/Probability-of-Dependent-and-Independent-Events-50000352/. This is a link to a 5-minute video of a teacher teaching the probability of independent and dependent events: http://nlvm.usu.edu/en/nav/frames_asid_305_g_3_t_5.html?from=category_g_3_t_5.html The National Library of Virtual Manipulatives coin toss probability application gives students a chance to practice, and it extends the lesson to graphing.
Reflection	Did my students reach the benchmark set by the standard 7.SP.C5: Understand that the probability of a chance event is a number between 0 and 1 that expresses the likelihood of the event occurring?

Table 2.4 Unpacking the Common Core State Standards Lesson Plan Template

Class	
Tier	
Standard(s)	
Guiding Questions	
Student-Friendly Objectives	
Academic Vocabulary	
Student Engagement	
Mini Lesson	
Differentiate	
Performance Task	
Assessment	
Technology Resources	
Reflection	

Looking closely at the lesson plan, we can see that each of the eight Standards for Mathematical Practice are exemplified in one or more of the activities:

1. Make sense of problems and persevere in solving them.
2. Reason abstractly and quantitatively.
3. Construct viable arguments and critique the reasoning of others.

4. Model with mathematics.

5. Use appropriate tools strategically.

6. Attend to precision.

7. Look for and make use of structure.

8. Look for and express regularity in repeated reasoning.

Take a moment to see if you can identify each Practice Standard in our sample lesson. Every unit of instruction should contain elements of the Standards for Mathematical Practice, though all eight standards may not be found in every individual lesson plan. A form to use as a checklist for the Practice Standards for your own lesson plans is found in Table 2.5.

Table 2.5   Standards for Mathematical Practice Checklist for My Unit Lesson Plan

Standard	*My Lesson Plan*
Make sense of problems and persevere in solving them.	
Reason abstractly and quantitatively.	
Construct viable arguments and critique the reasoning of others.	
Model with mathematics.	
Use appropriate tools strategically.	
Attend to precision.	
Look for and make use of structure.	
Look for and express regularity in repeated reasoning.	

Table 2.6 illustrates how our unit "Introduction to Probability of Independent and Compound Events" addresses the Standards for Mathematical Practice.

Table 2.6   Standards for Mathematical Practice Checklist for the Lesson Plan: Introduction to Probability of Independent and Compound Events

Standard	My Lesson Plan
Make sense of problems and persevere in solving them.	**Student-Friendly Objective:** Using hands-on inquiry, students will discover the rule for finding the probability of a single event and two independent events.
Reason abstractly and quantitatively.	**Mini Lesson 3:** Give each group of students a cardboard box representing a dresser draw with blue, green, red, white, and black paper "socks." Each pair is paper clipped together in a matching set. Have students reach into the sock drawer and choose a pair of socks without looking. Have them replace this pair and then choose another pair of socks. What is the probability that they will choose the red pair of socks both times?
Construct viable arguments and critique the reasoning of others.	Each student is given a different task in the group based on preferences and ability: a scribe to record the outcomes of the sock experiment using the mathematics vocabulary for the lesson, a "sock picker" to reach into the box with eyes closed to pick a pair of socks, a facilitator to lead the group discussion as they calculate the probability of picking each color after 10 events (the sock is replaced after each event), and the reporter that reports out to the class at the end of the experiment on how the group arrived at the answer. In this lesson, students use a hands-on approach to explore the probability of choosing a particular color pair of socks. Each student has an active role in the inquiry process.
Model with mathematics.	**Mini Lesson 2:** [Have] students pick a marble from a clear glass bowl containing five different color marbles and demonstrate how to calculate the probability of drawing a specific color marble. Then tell a story about the electricity going out and needing to take a pair of socks out of a drawer to wear with your green dress (or pants) without being able to see what color the socks are.
Use appropriate tools strategically.	**Assessment:** Have students flip a coin 20 times independently and calculate the probability of landing on heads.

Standard	My Lesson Plan
Attend to precision.	**Mini Lesson 4:** What is the probability (P) of choosing a green and then a yellow marble? $P \text{ (green)} = 1/5 \qquad P \text{ (yellow)} = 1/5$ $P \text{ (green and yellow)} = P \text{ (green)} \times P \text{ (yellow)}$ $1/5 \times 1/5 = 1/25 \qquad 1/25 = .04$ The probability of choosing a green marble and a yellow marble is 1/25, or .04.
Look for and make use of structure.	Students examine multiple experiments and create a rule for finding probability of multiple events.
Look for and express regularity in repeated reasoning.	**Mini Lesson 5:** Demonstrate one more example: The probability of landing on heads after tossing a coin *and* rolling a 5 on a single 6-sided die.

The new Common Core State Standards for mathematics provide a balance of understanding, fluency, and applications of mathematics. They are designed to support teachers and parents in helping students understand the importance of problem solving in mathematics and develop the skills to solve practical problems in the real world of the 21st century. RTI provides a structured framework for monitoring our students' growth as they master the essential elements of the CCSS. Together, this dynamic duo can leap the gaps in a single bound for all students, particularly students who struggle with mathematics.

The CCSS mathematics standards are available at www.corestandards .org/Math. The next section of this chapter provides some additional resources for further study.

Resources for Further Study

Learning to Read the Core: A View From 30,000 Feet

www.teachingchannel.org/videos/how-to-read-common-core

This site offers a very comprehensive video overview of the Common Core State Standards.

MasteryConnect Online Network for Teachers

www.masteryconnect.com

MasteryConnect is a network that teachers can join to share, review, and comment on assessment tools that align with the Common Core State Standards.

There is an option to follow members in the network and be notified of any postings from members in your network. Personalized reports can be generated with the paperless assessment tools, in which students can use their iPod, iPad, or Android device to fill in bubble sheets that are graded instantly. Results are reflected in a student-specific profile that indicates the level of performance according to a given Common Core standard or standards.

Common Core State Standards App for iPad and iPhone

https://itunes.apple.com/us/app/common-core-standards/
id439424555?mt=8

Using this app the reader can find standards by subject, grade, and subject category (domain/cluster). It includes math standards K–12 and language arts standards K–12. Math standards include both traditional and integrated pathways. The app is free at the time of this writing.

Mathematics Assessment Project

http://map.mathshell.org/materials/index.php

This website is the product of a collaboration between the Shell Center team at the University of Nottingham and the University of California, Berkeley. The project is designing and developing assessment tools to support schools in implementing the Common Core State Standards for mathematics. The site contains tools for formative and summative assessment, including performance goals required by CCSS. The prototype summative tests are designed to help teachers and students monitor their progress.

Tools and Activities for Teaching and Learning

http://iris.peabody.vanderbilt.edu/resources.html

This site contains web-based tools and activities that are designed to provide visual representations of mathematics concepts and assist students in seeing underlying patterns and recognizing critical elements, all of which are important for grasping math concepts (Ahmed, Clark-Jeavons, & Oldknow, 2004; Arcavi, 2003; Sloutsky & Yarlas, 2000).

Assisting Students Struggling With Mathematics: Response to Intervention (RTI) for Elementary and Middle Schools

http://ies.ed.gov/ncee/wwc/pdf/practiceguides/rti_math_pg_042109.pdf

This guide provides eight specific recommendations intended to help teachers, principals, and school administrators use Response to Intervention to identify students who need assistance in mathematics and to address the needs of these students through focused interventions. The guide provides suggestions on how to carry out each recommendation and explains how educators can overcome potential roadblocks to implementing the recommendations.

Common Core This Way

www.youtube.com/watch?v=BwND8J2SvGE

This is a YouTube video produced by Digigogy, running 4:21 minutes and using music to introduce the Common Core.

Math Common Core for Dummies

http://prezi.com/pr8cxffta7c7/math-common-core-for-dummies/

This guide was developed and published by Peri Nelson, a technology resource coordinator at the Oswego County (NY) Board of Cooperative Educational Services. It is an extremely beginner-friendly guide for anyone who may not be familiar with the Common Core State Standards and would like to learn more. It compares some of the old New York State MST standards with the CCSS. In addition to breaking down the standards into separate PK–8 and secondary categories, the site introduces terms such as *conceptual categories* and *clusters* that the audience may be unfamiliar with.

Tim Bedley's Elementary Math

www.rockinthestandards.com/tim/pages/teachers/common-core-standards/elementary-math.php

This website has videos that demonstrate the Common Core State Standards in mathematics in a classroom setting. It contains CCSS-aligned lesson plans.

Research Clips and Briefs

www.nctm.org/clipsandbriefs.aspx

In 2007, the National Council of Teachers of Mathematics launched Research Clips and Briefs. This resource helps teachers find research-based answers to questions about mathematics teaching and learning. Clips provide only the findings. Briefs include more information and list related research.

Glossary

Clusters: "Groups of related standards. Note that standards from different clusters may sometimes be closely related, because mathematics is a connected subject" (CCSSO, 2010, p. 5).

Coherence: "A progression of topics across grades [that] connects to other topics and vertical growth that reflects the nature of the discipline" (CCSSO, 2010, p. 5).

Domains: "Larger groups of related standards. Standards from different domains may sometimes be closely related" (CCSSO, 2010, p. 5).

Fluency: Speed and accuracy with simple calculations.

Focus: Identifies key ideas, understandings, and skills for each grade or course and stresses deep learning, which means applying concepts and skills within the same grade or course.

Rigor: Intensity.

Standards: "Define what students should understand and be able to do" (CCSSO, 2010, p. 5).

3

Universal Design and Mathematics

A Framework for RTI and Implementing the Common Core

By addressing the diversity of learners at the point of curriculum development (rather than as an afterthought or retrofit), Universal Design for Learning is a framework that enables educators to develop curricula that truly "leave no child behind" by maintaining high expectations for all students while effectively meeting diverse learning needs and monitoring student progress.

—CAST (1999–2012, para. 7)

In this chapter you will learn:

- A description of the brain-based research behind Universal Design for Learning (UDL)
- The principles of UDL
- Some specific examples demonstrating how to use the principles of UDL to assist struggling students to reach academic success as set by the Common Core State Standards (CCSS) benchmarks within a Response to Intervention (RTI) framework

Melissa Sun was a bright, active, sixth-grade girl who had struggled with mathematics since the first grade. Mrs. Guzzawitz was becoming increasingly concerned with Melissa's lack of progress in mathematics because new math skills continually build on previous knowledge. Early deficits can have enduring and devastating effects on later learning (National Council of Teachers of Mathematics [NCTM], 2000; National Mathematics Advisory Panel, 2008; U.S. Department of Education, 2003). Mrs. Guzzawitz decided to attend a professional development workshop on implementing the Common Core State Standards and RTI in her classroom using Universal Design for Learning as a framework to see if she might learn some strategies to help Melissa.

Brain-Based Research: A Word of Caution

The application of brain-based research to the study of human behavior—from politics and economics to psychology, education, literature, the fine arts, and even the culinary arts—has become an increasingly popular method for both research and practice (Lehrer, 2007). In education, the potential of neuroscience for understanding the learning process in children brings exciting new possibilities and challenges. Many of the ideas underlying this chapter are based on recent preliminary findings from brain research. However, we need to understand that these theories are still in their infancy and that reputable scientists and researchers have warned practitioners to apply them with caution. Reviewing the book *Aping Mankind: Neuromania, Darwinists and the Misrepresentation of Humanity*, by Raymond Tallis (2011), Andrew Scull (2012) remarked that

> much of the apparent plausibility of the neuromaniacs' claims, Tallis contends, rests on experiments that measure blood flow in the brain using magnetic resonance imaging. . . . [A] host of technical and conceptual flaws underlie this body of research, defects that vitiate any claim that people can trace the neural basis of complex thinking, let alone behavior. (p. 6)

As we explore the potential for brain science to help design more effective programs to teach mathematics, we offer similar words of caution.

Universal Design for Learning

Universal design, originally identified by the North Carolina State University Center for Universal Design (1997) and later expanded by the Center for Applied Special Technology (CAST), is an approach to the designing of instruction, assessment, materials, and content to benefit all students with different learning styles and abilities without adaptation or retrofitting. Its goal is to provide equal access to learning, not simply equal access to information. Universal design does not remove academic challenges; it removes barriers to access, participation, and progress in the general curriculum for all students. Universal design is just good teaching.

The fundamentals of Universal Design for Learning support the idea that students with disabilities, as well as typical students, fall along a continuum of learner differences. Teacher adjustments for learner differences should occur for all students, not just those with disabilities. Instead of remediating students so that they can learn from a set curriculum, curriculum, instruction materials, and strategies should be made flexible to accommodate learner differences in both general education and special education students (Rose & Meyer, 2000).

"UDL emphasizes that an effective goal must be flexible enough to allow learners multiple ways to successfully meet it. To do this, the standard must not embed the means (the how) with the goal (the what)" (CAST, 2011, para. 5). The Common Core State Standards for mathematics tell us what we want students to know and be able to do but not how we should go about teaching them. The standards are flexible enough so that all learners can meet a standard using their own pathway to success. The task of the classroom teacher is to create that pathway for each student.

Curriculum designers have long argued that what students know and what they can do depend on how the students first learned it (Shymansky, Marberry, & Jorgensen, 1977). Instruction that helps students learn mathematics with understanding, while actively building new knowledge from experience and old knowledge, can help remove barriers to student success (NCTM, 2000, p. 20). Instructional strategies such as explicitly teaching math concepts and overt instruction in the steps or procedures to solve a problem can also improve students' achievement in mathematics (Baker, Gersten, & Lee, 2002).

The Three Brain-Based Networks

UDL concepts are grounded in research on how the brain learns. MRI studies of the brain have identified different areas that become engaged when specific functions are performed. Neurons in the brain form networks that are interrelated and connect different parts of the brain into a system to perform the tasks at hand, including the tasks of learning. For example, MRI studies have found that, when someone carries out a planned movement, certain clusters of neurons in one area of the brain fire just before those in another area fire (Sousa, 2006). Neuroscientists have identified three major neural networks as having an important role in learning: the recognition network, the strategic network, and the affective network (Rose & Meyer, 2002). This chapter will examine some of the ways a teacher can engage these networks to help students learn the general curriculum, guided by the Common Core State Standards and the framework of Universal Design for Learning.

Tier 1: Removing Barriers for All Students

The *recognition network,* located in the center in the brain, processes the *what* of learning. It enables us to identify and understand information, ideas, and concepts. This network is specialized to sense and assign meaning to patterns we see, hear, taste, touch, and smell (Rose & Meyer, 2002). The underlying process causes us to identify things based on particular sensory experiences; this means that the quality of sensory input is very important. Poor lighting, low-quality photocopies, and mumbled speech can all impede processing and make recognition tasks difficult.

Teachers can remove these barriers to learning mathematics and improve processing within the recognition network by using some very simple strategies available in common word-processing applications such as Microsoft Word. For example, when creating practice worksheets of mathematics problems for students, some simple adjustments of the layout of problems on the page, such as adding spacing between the problems, can help to clarify the sensory input for students. Blank space on the worksheet (space on a page that is not occupied by text or graphics) is also helpful for some students. Using tables to organize space on a worksheet and providing structured space for solving problems eliminates visual confusion. Word-processing functions such as the ability to color-code or highlight important concepts and key phrases in sequential-step story problems are also helpful. Table 3.1 presents a format for a worksheet of word problems for a first-grade student that organizes space well.

Other strategies that engage the recognition network include providing examples, supplying samples of correctly solved problems, adding more visual and/or auditory input, and creating mathematics vocabulary lists with extra space for students to add their own examples or visual clues before teaching the concept that uses them. Identifying critical aspects of a mathematical concept engages the recognition network and may increase retention of those concepts or aspects. These strategies can be implemented without special training or materials; they have the potential to assist all students in learning mathematics and should be used in all tiers of an RTI program.

Using strategies that engage the recognition network is essential since mathematical thinking begins with the recognition of similarities among objects or events, proceeds to generalization and abstraction, and culminates in the ability to understand, explain, and make predictions (Rose & Meyer, 2002).

Table 3.1   Template for a Worksheet That May Reduce Visual Confusion for Some Students

Find the answer to this problem. Show a number sentence with your answer.	Draw a picture of your answer.
I saw 2 dogs on the lawn outside my bedroom window. How many legs did I see?	
There were 4 boys and 3 girls at Kyle's birthday party. How many children were at the party?	
My sister and I have 8 pieces of candy. If I have 3 pieces, how many pieces does my sister have?	

The *strategic network* in the brain focuses on the *how* of learning. It enables us to plan, execute, and self-monitor actions and skills. This network is specialized to generate and oversee mental and motor patterns (Rose & Meyer, 2002). The use of manipulatives, kinesthetic activities, and organizing material into smaller, more manageable units engages the strategic network. Identifying the underlying skills needed to solve a problem or understand a new concept and providing scaffolds in the form of partially solved problems or other supports facilitates the engagement of the strategic network. Expanding kinesthetic activities that provide opportunities for the student to do something during the lesson will also engage the strategic network.

The *affective network* is a center for understanding the *why* of learning. It is specialized to evaluate patterns and assign them emotional significance; it enables us to engage with tasks, learning, and the world around us (Rose & Meyer, 2002). Teaching mathematics to a struggling student in a way that engages the affective network makes the information meaningful and can remove some barriers to understanding. A mathematical concept presented in a context that provides connections to what the student already knows promotes mental imagery for mathematical ideas. Presenting new material using examples from the student's life promotes a familiar, comfortable feeling for the new learning. Opportunities for communication between the student and teacher, or among students, about the lesson also engages the affective network. This is especially important when we are teaching students with diverse backgrounds or those for whom English is not a first language.

The number of problems or pages assigned in a mathematics activity should match individual capabilities so as not to overwhelm or upset the student, which is likely to produce a negative response within the affective network of the brain. Sometimes, less is more. Often, a few problems with guided practice, including teacher feedback, can help students rehearse the mathematics process or concept and move it from short-term memory to long-term memory (Rosenshine, 2012). Teachers should also consider assigning mathematical exercises that have an appropriate balance of challenge and support (Hitchcock, Meyer, Rose, & Jackson, 2002). The level of challenge and rigor of the assignment should be within what Vygotsky (1934/1978) has identified as the zone of proximal development; that is, just beyond reach but obtainable with effort (Hitchcock et al., 2002). Problems that are too challenging negatively affect the student's self-efficacy and consequently engage the affective network in a negative way. Instruction with partially solved problems on a worksheet, or modeled by the teacher, can scaffold the student's skills to solve the more rigorous problems required by the CCSS.

The brain processes emotional, as well as cognitive, data during learning. If the student responds negatively to a situation, the complex cognitive functions can be curtailed or even suspended. This makes learning new material difficult, if not impossible (Sousa, 2006). Engaging the affective network in a positive way can enhance the student's opportunities for learning and retention of new mathematical concepts and ideas.

Principles of Universal Design

The North Carolina State University Center for Universal Design (1997) created a framework of seven original principles for planning instruction aligned with universal design:

1. Equitable use

2. Flexibility in use

3. Simple and intuitive use

4. Perceptible information

5. Tolerance for error

6. Low physical effort

7. Size and space for approach and use

The work of Scott, McGuire, and Shaw (2003) expands this basic group to include two additional principles: *a community of learners* and a *welcoming and inclusive environment*.

The discussion that follows examines the use of this framework specifically in implementing the Common Core State Standards for mathematics.

Principle 1: *Equitable Use*—This ensures that the design is useful to people with diverse abilities. The design of instructional activities and materials should be appealing. Technology can be helpful to facilitate multiple media (podcasts, video, etc.) for access to instruction on a topic based on the students' interest and skills. The same concept can be presented in text (textbook, worksheet, etc.) or streaming video. Streaming video that teaches mathematical content is available free or at little cost. For example, PBS produced and distributes a series called *Cyberchase* (http://pbskids.org/cyber chase), which includes online interactive resources, printable worksheets, and video segments. Lesson plans are provided with specific mathematical content and objectives are identified and aligned to the Common Core State Standards for mathematics as well as *The Principals and Standards for School Mathematics* (NCTM, 2000). Additional resources are found at the end of this chapter.

Principle 2: *Flexibility in Use*—Instruction should provide opportunities for choice. Teachers can give students a structured choice of media to solve a problem (use of either virtual manipulatives, such as those found at http://nlvm.usu.edu/en/nav/vlibrary.html, or paper and pencil to draw a picture of the problem). Other ways of implementing Principle 2 include providing students with a choice of different but equal assignments and adapting assignments to the user's pace, as described in the discussion of Vygotsky's (1934/1978) work.

Principle 3: *Simple and Intuitive Use*—This addresses the need to eliminate unnecessary complexity in instructions in mathematics assignments. Teaching mathematics using "big ideas" instead of rote memorization of the algorithm and providing exemplars of correctly solved problems align mathematics instruction with this principle. The teaching of big ideas is a foundation of the Common Core. For example, rather than teaching students how to solve a problem, teachers need to think of ways to use a problem to teach the mathematics of a unit or concept: focus lessons on major topics, pursue conceptual understanding, develop procedural skill and fluency, and application of the mathematics to a real-world problem the student can identify with.

Principle 4: *Perceptible Information*—This addresses the communication of information, regardless of the student's sensory abilities. It involves increasing the legibility of essential information by using different and redundant forms of presentation (pictorial, verbal, tactile). As described earlier, the functions of simple word processors are particularly useful in this type of differentiation (e.g., changing the size of the font, leaving more space on a page, using tables to organize the space on a page of problems).

Principle 5: *Tolerance for Error*—This minimizes hazards and errors through practices such as assessing students' current level of competence and prerequisite skills, teacher-guided practice, frequent formative assessment, and adjusting instruction and scaffolds to facilitate student success on an assignment. Using technology such as Chart Dog 2.0 (www.jimwright online.com/php/chartdog_2_0/chartdog.php) for progress monitoring can help to target instruction. Providing partially solved problems as scaffolds, as described previously, is another way of implementing this principle and enhancing the instruction of important mathematical concepts.

Principle 6: *Low Physical Effort*—This supports the design of mathematics instruction to minimize repetitive actions. This is particularly important when the repeated actions include errors. Prompting and feedback during and after task completion will help to lower the rate of repeated errors in solving mathematical problems or operations. Repetitive wrong responses to a problem may facilitate moving the wrong process or algorithm from the student's short-term memory into long-term memory or tire or reduce the student's enthusiasm or engagement. Computer-assisted programs can give the student immediate feedback on responses and minimize the opportunity to develop incorrect problem-solving approaches. And of course, careful monitoring by the teacher is always very effective. Sometimes, giving a student 5 or 10 problems to do can be more effective than giving him or her 25—sometimes less is more.

Principle 7: *Size and Space for Approach and Use*—This reminds us to provide a clear line of sight to important instructional elements such as the blackboard or SMART Board. Place computer screens at appropriate heights, and demonstrate instructional materials or manipulatives in a way that all students in the class can see. If students need assistive devices, adequate space should be provided. And the teacher should always face students when speaking.

Principal 8: *Community of Learners*—This promotes interaction and communication among students in study groups and provides opportunities for collaborative problem solving in cooperative learning groups. This can have multiple benefits for students (see Chapter 5 for strategies). Additional information about the benefits of communication in mathematics can also be found at www.nctm.org/standards/content.aspx?menu_id=1155 &id=26872.

Principle 9: *Welcoming and Inclusive Environment*—Hold high expectations for all students and implement a zero tolerance policy for negativity. Assessments, like instruction, should provide multiple media and opportunities for students to demonstrate what they know. The teacher can use that information to target direct instruction, as needed, for both the new skill being assessed and the prerequisite skills needed as a foundation for learning the new mathematical concept (see Chapter 4).

Source: Based on *Principles of Universal Design for Instruction,* by Sally S. Scott, Joan M. McGuire, and Stan F. Shaw, Center on Postsecondary Education and Disability, University of Connecticut. Copyright 2001. Reprinted and adapted with permission.

After learning about brain-based learning and UDL in her professional development workshop, Mrs. Guzzawitz taught lessons on calculating volume. She administered a probe on finding the volume of a cube or rectangular prism. The results showed Melissa and three other students had not mastered the concept of calculating volume. After meeting with the RTI team, it was decided to move Melissa and the other struggling students to Tier 2. Here, Melissa received 30 minutes of instruction in addition to her regular classroom mathematics instruction focusing on Common Core State Standard, Grade 6 Geometry. The instruction took place in class twice a week in a small-group setting that included the three other students struggling with the same concepts. While Melissa and the three other students worked in a group with a teaching assistant, Mrs. Guzzawitz circulated around the room, giving feedback to the other students in the class who were working on worksheets that reinforced the day's lesson. With the help of a teaching assistant, Melissa's group used the computers in the classroom to access an online lesson (http://illuminations.nctm.org/LessonDetail.aspx?ID=L831) that uses an interactive applet to investigate the formula for the volume of a rectangular prism. It also encourages students to construct two origami boxes and use centimeter cubes to measure and compare the volume of the boxes. The student activities on the website engage each of the three primary networks: recognition, strategic, and affective.

To address the recognition network, Mrs. Guzzawitz used easy-to-read handouts with words (cubic centimeters, space inside, etc.) and basic shapes (cube and rectangular solid) identified that helped Melissa and the other students use prior knowledge to understand and benefit from the activity.

To address the strategic network, she used a formula page template created for the students with pictures of shapes, definitions of key words present on the formulas (e.g., *length, width, side*), and the formulas for each figure.

To address the affective network, Mrs. Guzzawitz provided an additional handout with organized steps for the students to follow in order to help them organize their actions to solve the guided practice problems. Some steps she suggested were drawing a picture, rewriting the formula, highlighting important information (e.g., measurements of dimensions to be used), and giving answers in completes sentences, not just in numbers. She used volume problems in a context Melissa could relate to or that utilize items present in the classroom or at Melissa's home.

> If Melissa was still challenged after 6 weeks, she would be moved to Tier 3. Here, she would receive individual instruction for 30 minutes three times a week and an individualized instruction plan, focused on her unique needs, that would address the barriers to her success.
>
> This would be done using an Excel spreadsheet or a Word table. The plan would include materials and methods currently in use (e.g., textbooks, calculators, drawings, printed handouts), potential barriers to Melissa's use of these materials (e.g., difficulty reading small text, lack of drawing skills, difficulty keeping track of steps, difficulty working alone), and new solutions for these barriers during the lesson (e.g., partially filled-in handouts, physical shapes for students to touch and trace, graphic programs to create better visuals, real-life examples; Rose & Meyer, 2002).

For struggling students like Melissa, a documented examination of barriers in conjunction with progress monitoring data can be very helpful to a teacher or team designing effective interventions. Table 3.2 shows an example of a template for a UDL RTI intervention plan.

A sample template of possible solutions to overcome barriers using the three networks that are the foundation of the UDL approach to instruction follows in Table 3.3.

Fortunately, Mellissa was able to achieve mastery after 4 weeks in Tier 2. When the team met and analyzed the data collected through progress monitoring, it was decided that she could return to Tier 1 whole-class instruction.

Table 3.2   Template for an RTI UDL Tiered Intervention Plan

RTI UDL Tiered Intervention Plan Name:

Lesson Topic:

Objectives:

Targeted Common Core State Standard(s):

Language or Other Barriers:

Vocabulary Words:

Assessments (Prior Knowledge and Ongoing):

Solutions Using the Recognition Network	*Solutions Using the Strategic Network*	*Solutions Using the Affective Network*
Tier 1		
Tier 2		
Tier 3		

Table 3.3   Solutions to Overcome Barriers Using Instructional Strategies Based on the Three Networks

Solutions Using the Recognition Network	Solutions Using the Strategic Network	Solutions Using the Affective Network
Tier 1 Barrier: Difficulty in reading small text, difficulty working alone Use large fonts on worksheets.	Begin instruction with simplest concepts and move to more complex. Use manipulatives that can build three-dimensional forms.	Develop partners. Use think, pair, share strategy.
Tier 2 Model solutions and use podcasts or videos to present material.	Use a formula page template as a scaffold with pictures of shapes, definitions, and formulas.	Use small-group instruction with teacher-guided practice.
Tier 3 Use multiple forms of presentation: pictorial, verbal, tactile.	Use virtual manipulatives of three-dimensional forms. Provide opportunities for student verbalization of thought processes.	Give individual instruction.

Universal Design for Learning can be implemented with or without the use of technology and provides a framework for teachers to engage and teach all their students. The effective teaching of mathematics in the elementary grades is essential to student success in mathematics throughout the students' later academic career. A lack of fluency and understanding of basic mathematical concepts and the big ideas in mathematics during the elementary grade builds an insurmountable barrier to the understanding of mathematics in high school and subsequently throughout life. More details regarding the conceptual focus of instruction in each grade level is found in Chapter 2. Universal Design for Learning will not solve all of the difficulties that some students face, but it can be a solution for a great many of these difficulties. Teachers can use these principles at any level, including high school or college. On a larger scale, UDL provides a framework for success in a diverse society that can allow students to prosper, provided equal opportunities are available. It is our right and our responsibility as educators to provide that opportunity.

The sample lesson ideas that follow use universal design as a theoretical framework, are guided by the Common Core State Standards for mathematics, and take UDL from theory to practice.

Ideas for Common Core Lessons That Implement Universal Design for Learning: Lessons That Include Strategies in RTI Tier 1

MEASURE THE TEDDY BEAR

CCSS Grade 1 Measurement and Data: Measure lengths indirectly and by iterating length units

www.apples4theteacher.com/measure.html

This site contains an interactive online game called Measure the Teddy Bear. It consists of 10 questions, each worth 10 points. Each question shows the teddy doing different activities in relationship to the ruler he is standing with. The student must go through the series of activities and measure the teddy 10 times. Sound effects and colorful graphics make it appropriate for beginner's mathematics.

IDENTIFYING POLYGONS

CCSS Grade 2 Geometry: Reason with shapes and their attributes

The features of polygons are foundational mathematical concepts for many topics addressed in elementary and secondary mathematics. An elementary teacher, aligning instruction with universal design, might demonstrate different paper examples of polygons in different orientations with the number of sides identified. To engage the strategic network, students could be asked to draw polygons and shapes that are not polygons. To engage the affective network, software or video clips, especially with audio narration (e.g., www.youtube.com/watch?v=TTrbT_SSDOU), may also be helpful. The lesson could engage the recognition network by including a homework assignment that requires the student to identify polygons in the real world.

PLACE VALUE INTERACTIVE STYLE!

CCSS Grade 4 Number & Operations in Base 10: Generalize place value understanding for multi-digit whole numbers

Place value is an important concept in the Common Core, beginning with the foundation skills addressed in kindergarten and in the NCTM (2000) number and operations standards.

This lesson is designed to reinforce the concept of place value up to 10,000. The lesson plan assumes the concept has already been introduced, and the activity provides practice engaging the three networks identified in UDL.

The lesson uses tennis balls and four small plastic waste paper baskets taped together. Each basket has a label that designates it as a basket of 1s, 10s, 100s, or 1,000s. Students are grouped into three-person teams: one to shoot the ball, one to move the baskets back and forth, and one to keep score. Each team is allowed as many shots as necessary to make nine baskets. The score keeper identifies where the balls land and the number that represents their combined place value. For example, if the team has four balls drop in the 1,000s, four balls drop in the 10s, and one ball drops in the 1s, their score would be 4041. The winner is decided after all teams finish, and a random draw out from a hat determines if high overall score or low overall score is the winning team. Watching other teams as they play the game helps to even the playing field and holds students' interest. In addition, the rule for determining the winner prevents one team from setting the basket so that all their nine baskets count as 1,000s or as 1s.

In this activity all three networks of UDL are addressed:

- The recognition network (the *what* of learning) is addressed by displaying the place value score card and by displaying the value of each place value basket.
- The strategic network (the *how* of the lesson) is addressed by the students throwing the balls, followed by observing which basket they land in, and recording the results.
- The affective network (the *why* of the lesson) is addressed by the students' engagement in the game. The hands-on approach and the anticipation of all students, as the winning team will not be known until the end, promote the students' engagement in the task. As a review at the end of the class, the teacher can then follow up with a short video on place value (www.youtube.com/watch?v=963IUfaH7b0).

Tier 2: Strategies for Focused Group Instruction

Tier 2 interventions use systematic, explicit methods; skills and concepts begin with the most simple, moving to the more complex, guided by ongoing assessment results. Explicit instructional methods, including teacher modeling, teacher-guided student practice, and student independent practice with frequent feedback, are part of most Tier 2 interventions.

Tier 2 interventions should differ from Tier 1 in the following aspects: additional time beyond regular classroom instruction, different research-based instructional strategies, focus on small-group instruction, and different materials. In a study of Tier 2 interventions for a group of first and second graders identified as having difficulties in mathematics, the interventions consisted of 60–65 sessions (in addition to regular classroom instruction), of 15 minutes each, over a period of 18 weeks in small groups of three to four students of similar ability. The concepts addressed in the study were number concepts and relationships (i.e., magnitude, number identification and writing, numeric sequencing and counting), base 10, and place value. The results show positive improvement for the students in the study (Bryant, Bryant, Gersten, Scammacca, Funk et al., 2008).

Let's examine a possible Tier 2 intervention for place value, a concept found in the CCSS for Grades K–5. We will focus on an intervention for a single student.

To get a better understanding of the student's prior knowledge, the teacher may wish to interview the student before choosing a specific Tier 2 intervention.

For example, if the student had not mastered place value in Tier 1, in addition to the regular assessments, the following short interview questions may shed light on where to start:

- I am going to write some numbers. Can you say them for me? (54, 945, 23, 456, 734, 945)
- How many tens are there in 60? In 6,000?
- Write a very large number and then say it.

The interview is done in addition to the regular assessment protocol to help target the intervention. Let's begin by looking at the three key elements of place value identified by Ross (1989):

1. The values represented by individual digits are determined by their positions in numbers.

2. The value of an individual digit is found by multiplying its face value by the multiple of 10 assigned to that position.

3. The quantity represented by the whole number is the sum of the values of these individual digits.

Another evidence-based strategy to teach place value is the place value development method identified by Ross (1989), which includes the *face value construct* (the mistaken belief, held by some students, that each digit in a multi-digit number is independent of the others and actually represents only its face value). For example, a student may erroneously see the expression 431 as a collection of three independent numbers that equal 8 (4 + 3 + 1), instead of a single number that could be expressed as 400 + 30 + 1. Since grouping is the foundation for understanding place value, we will start there and move from the simple to the complex (systematic, explicit methods) and create a lesson activity that will reinforce and teach this skill.

To engage the three networks, we can start the lesson with a story that we have invented a new flavor of ice cream that can be produced only in cubes.

Our ice cream flavor, called Cubo, has been advertised on TV, and we have just received our first order for 135 cubes. We need to ship the ices cream in boxes. We will use our base-10 blocks, shown in Figure 3.1, to represent the Cubos.

Base-10 blocks consist of cubes (1s place), rods (10s place), flats (100s place), and blocks (1,000s place). The teacher will have a group of 135 base-10 blocks and model Cubo packaged with the following: 5 individual cubes, three sets of 10 cubes (long packages), and one set of 100 cubes (flat packages).

Figure 3.1   Base-10 Blocks

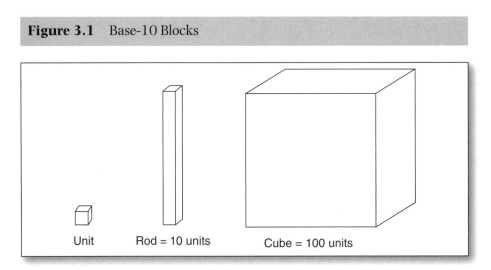

Unit   Rod = 10 units   Cube = 100 units

Ask the students in their groups to use the base-10 blocks to find other ways of packing the Cubo ice cream in boxes for shipment. (They can use more long boxes or more individual boxes, etc.) If there are four members in a group, two members will be scribes and draw the different ways that they could fill orders for 135 cubes, and two members will move the base-10 blocks around to explore solutions. Numbers of group members can change based on which students are available for the lesson. Try this with several three-digit numbers and have the group report out their solutions. Reverse the process and have the students come up with a three-digit number and create shipment boxes for that number. Then ask the students to create boxes for multiples of 10 (i.e., 100, 10, and 1). Use the same number that the students used in the hands-on exercise, and write them in tables such as Table 3.4.

As closure to this lesson you may wish to play the song found at www .youtube.com/watch?v=5W47G-h7myY.

After administering an assessment on mastery up to 100s, the students can then move on to 1000s. Following this, the teacher can use bundles of straws divided into tens, hundreds, and thousands in the same way as the base-10 cubes to demonstrate concrete representation of the value of the digits in each position.

Table 3.4   Table for Place Value Numbers

100s	10s	1s

Tier 3: Strategies for Intensive Individual Intervention

Tier 3 intervention is the most intensive stage within RTI. It is focused on individual students, and its components must include instruction in evidence-based curricula, implementation of interventions with fidelity to the RTI process, and analysis of outcomes using formative and summative assessment data. It is usually administered by someone with advanced training. As in Tier 2, there is strong evidence that instruction during this intervention should be explicit and systematic (Gersten, Chard et al., 2009). This includes providing models of proficient problem solving, verbalization of thought processes, guided practice, corrective feedback, and frequent cumulative review. Interventions should include instruction on solving word problems that is based on common underlying structures, such as recognizing problems with similar patterns and representation (e.g., a rate problem; Gersten, Chard et al., 2009). Tier 3 interventions should be based on the end point of Tier 2, individualized to the particular student, and aligned with the constructs of Universal Design for Learning and the Common Core.

There is no silver bullet to help teachers reach all students in every concept of every lesson. The principles of universal design, identified by the Center for Universal Design at North Carolina State University, involve an understanding of the three networks that are the foundation of Universal Design for Learning and provide guidelines that are consistent and aligned with the *Principles and Standards for School Mathematics* (NCTM, 2000), the Common Core State Standards for mathematics content and practices, and the three tiers of RTI. These concepts can help teachers reach all their students using multiple means of engagement, learning, and assessment. The use of assessment data, essential to RTI implementation, is a fundamental component of any instructional strategy within any program based on RTI, NCTM standards, or the Common Core. While not highlighted in this chapter, the reader will see that the methods presented on progress monitoring (see Chapter 4) can be used to assess the effect of UDL strategies on student learning of a concept. The principles of UDL help us create lessons that engage the three brain-based networks to increase the probability of a student's success in mathematics. Instruction that implements multiple learning principles increases the likelihood of engaging multiple pathways in the student's brain. The more passages the student engages while learning fundamental mathematical concepts, the more likely the student will retain the concepts he or she has learned (Sousa, 2006). It should be noted that many of the "new initiatives" are not completely new ideas but simply examples of fundamental, time-honored teaching skills that take effort to do well in order to benefit kids in a student-centered classroom. Integrating RTI, UDL, and the Common Core creates an effective balance of content and habits of practice.

 Tech Byte

C A S T

www.cast.org

The UDL framework uses instructional methods, materials, and assessments that are differentiated to address the diverse needs of students by engaging each of the three networks of the brain. One way for teachers to implement UDL into their classrooms is to use resources and tools from the CAST website that utilize UDL principles. This resource contains modules, sample lesson plans, tutorials, and UDL software available to teachers and administrators looking to incorporate UDL into their models.

The CAST website has various components: UDL research, professional development, and learning tools. Examples of these learning tools include book builder programs, curriculum guidelines, and a strategy tutor (supported by Google), which assists students with reading and writing.

After signing up for a free account, users can click on the Learning Tools link, which connects them to a list of links for various UDL learning tool items. One interesting tool that has many applications, particularly in mathematics, is the CAST UDL Curriculum Self-Check. This gives teachers the ability to take their existing curriculum and lessons and check them against the UDL system to ensure that there is flexibility to reach all students. This tool is helpful in the RTI framework as well, because teachers can use it to develop lessons in the three tiers that are scaffolded and flexible enough to reach all learners, including those in need of support.

The CAST UDL Curriculum Self-Check is divided into three specific areas: (1) Learn About Universal Design for Learning (UDL), (2) Check Your Curriculum, and (3) Explore Resources. In Learn About UDL, the site offers videos, literature, and activities to give the teacher background knowledge about UDL (see Figure 3.2).

Figure 3.2   CAST UDL Curriculum Self-Check: Learn About Universal
Design for Learning

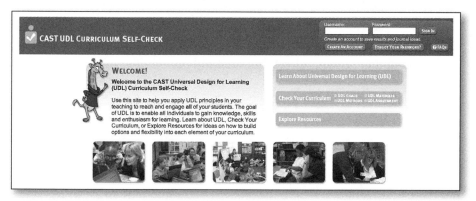

Source: © CAST, 2013. http://udlselfcheck.cast.org

The second part, Check Your Curriculum, is a more in-depth software
tool which allows teachers to check different areas of their curriculum for
UDL accessibility. Users can choose between three online coaches to help
them evaluate their curriculum. They can then access the coach when
evaluating their own lesson or unit. The Check Your Curriculum module
includes four areas: UDL Goals, UDL Methods, UDL Materials, and UDL
Assessment (see Figure 3.3).

Figure 3.3   CAST UDL Curriculum Self-Check: Check Your Curriculum

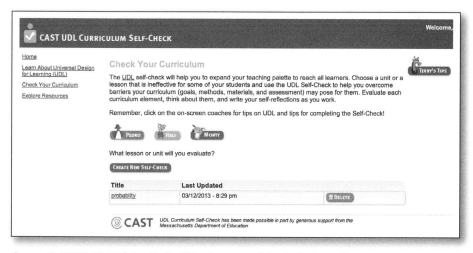

Source: © CAST, 2013. http://udlselfcheck.cast.org/check.php?op=edit

Clicking on the link accesses one of the curriculum sections, where users are brought to a page on which they can assess their own goals (or methods, materials, or assessment) using UDL's criteria and assess their understandings of students' goals (or methods, materials, or assessments) in relation to the lesson created. There is also a section for self-reflection. One distinctive feature found throughout the UDL body of software is the character that offer tips that users can click on throughout the process. The characters give suggestions on how to make the curriculum more accessible to students with diverse learning needs (see Figure 3.3). The next screen, accessible by clicking on Create New Self-Check, enables users to see a sample curriculum, in this case, probability. Figure 3.4 shows the modules that will lead users through the adaptation of the curriculum.

The CAST website allows teachers to use existing plans and curriculum, adapting and scaffolding them to make them accessible to students using the principles and framework of RTI. Mathematics teachers can use a tool like this as a self-check system to ensure they are reaching all of their students and teaching for a diverse student population.

Figure 3.4   CAST UDL Curriculum Self-Check: Check Your Curriculum: UDL Goal

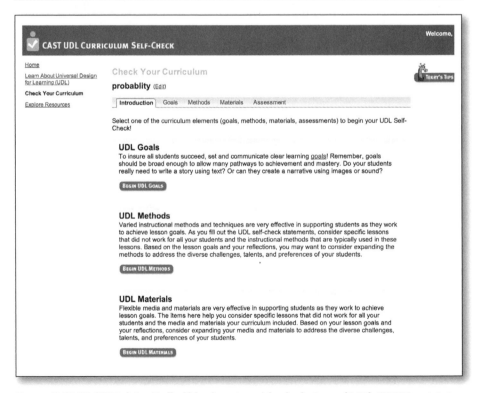

Source: © CAST, 2013. http://udlselfcheck.cast.org/check.php?op=edit&id=8057&sect=intro

Resources for Further Learning

Berkas, N., & Pattison, C. (2008, April). Differentiated Instruction and Universal Design for Learning. *NCTM News Bulletin.*

www.nctm.org/news/release_list.aspx?id=14867

This article gives an overview of the relationship between differentiated instruction and RTI.

Interactivate

www.shodor.org/interactivate/

This website has over 150 Java-based interactive tools and activities (aka, applets), categorized by topic, that allow students to explore mathematics. It's a free resource developed and maintained by the Shodor Educational Foundation for teachers and students. All the tools and activities have explanations for how to use them in the classroom, and most are aligned with common math texts. All are aligned to the NCTM standards and the Common Core State Standards for mathematics.

UDL Guidelines in Practice: Grade 1 Mathematics

www.youtube.com/watch?v=KuTJJQWnMaQ

In this video, a panel of UDL experts takes you inside a diverse classroom to show master teachers applying the principles and guidelines of UDL in a lesson on estimating.

Edyburn, D. L. (2009). Response to Intervention (RTI): Is There a Role for Assistive Technology?

www.setp.net/articles/article0903-1.html

This article discusses the relationship of RTI to Universal Design for Learning and assistive technology.

Strategies to Improve Access to the General Education Curriculum

www.k12.wa.us/specialed/programreview/monitoring/Placement/StrategiestoImproveAccess.pdf

This extensive online resource comes in the form of a downloadable PDF file that includes a large annotated list of free web-based mathematics tools and activities developed by CAST for The Access Center: Improving Outcomes for All Students K–8.

4 Progress Monitoring

Avoiding a Blind Date With Data

John Kappenberg and Harold J. Dean

"Would you tell me, please, which way I ought to go from here?"

"That depends a good deal on where you want to get to," said the Cat.

"I don't much care where—" said Alice.

"Then it doesn't matter which way you go," said the Cat.

"—so long as I get SOMEWHERE," Alice added as an explanation.

"Oh, you're sure to do that," said the Cat, "if you only walk long enough."

—Lewis Carroll, *Alice's Adventures in Wonderland*

In this chapter you will learn:

- A definition of progress monitoring
- The research on progress monitoring and mathematics
- How to progress monitor
- The outcomes from progress monitoring
- Progress monitoring, as it relates to Response to Intervention and the Common Core State Standards

Raphael is a 10-year-old student in Ms. Diaz's fourth-grade class. His teacher describes him as a student who "works very hard, tries very hard, and earns the grades he gets." In his class of 26 students, Raphael places near the 50th percentile in literacy but below the 20th in mathematics. He was in another school district until halfway through the third grade, and his attendance was inconsistent for the final 5 months that year. His previous year's teacher, Mr. Klein, noted that Raphael's scores had a great deal of fluctuation on mathematic assessment probes. Mr. Klein flagged him as at-risk when he performed at "low average/ borderline below average" level on the school's spring benchmark assessments in fluency with whole number operations, addition, subtraction, multiplication, and division. Raphael's scores in the geometry area were "average."

Raphael's school has implemented the new, more rigorous Common Core State Standards (CCSS) in mathematics. Ms. Diaz was concerned about Raphael's progress so far in mathematics and building a foundation for higher mathematics in the upper grades, which is guided by the three critical areas of the fourth-grade focus of the CCSS:

1. developing understanding and fluency with multi-digit multiplication, and developing understanding of dividing to find quotients involving multi-digit dividends

2. developing an understanding of fraction equivalence, addition and subtraction of fractions with like denominators, and multiplication of fractions by whole numbers

3. understanding that geometric figures can be analyzed and classified based on their properties, such as having parallel sides, perpendicular sides, particular angle measures, and symmetry. (Council of Chief State School Officers, 2010, p. 27)

Upon reviewing Raphael's assessment results from third grade and those administered in the fall of fourth grade, Ms. Diaz was able to narrow down some areas in which Raphael needed specific support. On the fourth-grade benchmark assessment, he achieved appropriate mastery in addition and subtraction. To address Rafael's difficulty with multiplication and division, Ms. Diaz decided to develop an intervention strategy to help Raphael and monitor how he responded to the intervention(s) using a systematic assessment approach known as *progress monitoring*.

What Is Progress Monitoring?

Progress monitoring (PM) is "an empirically developed approach to formative evaluation that relies on frequent assessment using brief measures that serve as indicators of general proficiency in a content area" (Foegen, 2008, p. 69). This process uses frequent and brief (often 1- to 5-minute) measures to inform teachers and guide instruction.

Research on Progress Monitoring and Mathematics

As the Common Core State Standards are implemented and Response to Intervention (RTI) becomes part of the classroom teacher's routine, so does the process of monitoring student progress and outcomes. Of course, traditionally, teachers have administered tests and quizzes to see if their class has understood a concept or can accurately complete mathematical problems. But progress monitoring in the RTI framework is different. In the RTI framework, assessment has a distinct and defined purpose as a process for periodically and scientifically evaluating student performance across time, with the data used to judge whether an intervention is achieving the expected results (National Association of State Directors of Special Education, 2005). The screening and assessment measures used in progress monitoring can also serve as predictors for student achievement (Fuchs et al., 2007).

How to "Progress Monitor"

Given the frequency of tests and quizzes, homework checks, and students completing problems on the board in many classrooms, progress monitoring data seem to be everywhere. True, but are they the right data and are we using them to guide (i.e., make changes in) our instruction, rather than simply assess how our students are doing? Are we using data we collect to tell us whether our students are moving toward mastery of a skill, a concept, a theme, or a curriculum, and if they are not, are we changing our own approach to instruction in response? Oftentimes, our traditional approach to assessment has not been particularly geared to diagnosing student difficulties. Classroom tests are usually given at the end of a unit of study, but waiting until the end of a unit to discover that a student isn't learning may be too late for remediation. Random quizzes give us only snapshots and don't necessarily show growth. Homework is affected by too many external factors, such as uncertainty over who actually completed the work and what level of support the student received.

If a teacher is to know whether students are benefitting from instruction, data must be collected and analyzed systematically in ways that yield specific and cumulative information about a student. This needs to occur early in the teaching process, not days or weeks later. The information should then be used to guide instruction (Mellard & Johnson, 2008). Progress monitoring is a systematic method used in the RTI process to assess student learning at frequent intervals (National Center on Student Progress Monitoring, n.d.). It allows the teacher to determine whether instruction is benefitting the students, and it informs decisions about students who are not benefitting appropriately (Fisher & Frey, 2010; Fuchs & Fuchs, 2006). Let's return to Ms. Diaz and Rafael.

> Ms. Diaz decided to work for 10 minutes daily with Raphael and several other students that were struggling with the mathematics content, reviewing or preteaching the day's concept in mathematics. Given this Tier 1 intervention, Ms. Diaz set a goal in mathematics performance after 18 weeks that she felt was appropriate for Raphael, which included intermediate goals. The goal shown here identifies the intervention interval, the points she expected him to achieve, and the progress monitoring probes to be used for assessment.

Given that the K–5 CCSS are designed to provide students with a "solid foundation in whole numbers, addition, subtraction, multiplication, and division" (Common Core State Standards Initiative, 2012, para. 1), and considering Raphael's appropriate scores on the addition and subtraction

> **Mathematics Goal:** By the winter benchmark assessment (6 weeks), Raphael will write 18 correct digits out of 36 in 4 minutes on nine multi-digit whole number multiplication problems. By the spring benchmark assessment (12 weeks), Raphael will write 36 correct digits out of 36 in 4 minutes.

probes, Ms. Diaz's intervention was going to focus on the two operations of multiplication and division with whole numbers. She decided that her strategy would be to work on Raphael's multiplication skills first, then move to an intervention for division. During regular class instruction, Ms. Diaz worked to have all the students reach the benchmark fourth-grade goal for Operations and Algebraic Thinking (Table 4.1) by the end of the school year.

> Ms. Diaz implemented the typical Tier 1 intervention steps in an RTI model:
>
> - She identified the student through a screening or benchmark assessment.
> - She reviewed performance data to determine a specific area of focus.
> - She selected an intervention strategy to address the specific area or areas she would focus on.
> - She set a goal to help in planning for growth toward mastery.
> - She selected a measurement tool to monitor the student's progress.
>
> Ms. Diaz would then deliver the intervention as described above to Raphael and monitor how he responded using a systematic assessment approach known as progress monitoring.

Table 4.1 Common Core State Standards: Grade 4 Operations and Algebraic Thinking 4.OA

Use the four operations with whole numbers to solve problems.	
4.1	Interpret a multiplication equation as a comparison, e.g., interpret $35 = 5 \times 7$ as a statement that 35 is 5 times as many as 7 and 7 times as many as 5. Represent verbal statements of multiplicative comparisons as multiplication equations.
4.2	Multiply or divide to solve word problems involving multiplicative comparison, e.g., by using drawings and equations with a symbol for the unknown number to represent the problem, distinguishing multiplicative comparison from additive comparison.
4.3	Solve multi-step word problems posed with whole numbers and having whole-number answers using the four operations, including problems in which remainders must be interpreted. Represent these problems using equations with a letter standing for the unknown quantity. Assess the reasonableness of answers using mental computation and estimation strategies including rounding.

Source: © Copyright 2010. National Governors Association Center for Best Practices and Council of Chief State School Officers. All rights reserved.

Because progress monitoring (PM) is a systematic approach, it is best implemented using the predefined six basic steps noted in Table 4.2 as they relate to mathematics and RTI (Iowa Department of Education, 2006).

Table 4.2 Six Basic Steps of Progress Monitoring

1. **Define the behavior.**	Describe the measurable skill that is the goal of the curriculum unit, and the change in the student's performance needed to reach the goal in the set time.
2. **Select the measurement strategy.**	Define the method used to monitor the student's performance.
3. **Establish a baseline.**	Describe the student's level of performance before instruction, or intervention, begins.
4. **Create a goal.**	Describe the measureable level of performance required for mastery of the skill or concept.
5. **Develop a chart or graph.**	Define the method for plotting data to illustrate the student's progress throughout the unit.
6. **Create a decision-making plan.**	Develop a strategy for deciding what form of data will be collected and how often, how it will be analyzed, and what critical evidence will be accepted as indicators that a change in intervention is needed.

Source: Burton & Kappenberg (2012, p. 25).

STEP 1. DEFINE THE BEHAVIOR: WHAT DO MY STUDENTS NEED TO LEARN?

The most commonly used term to describe the measurement process in progress monitoring is *curriculum-based measurement* (CBM) (Hosp, Hosp, & Howell, 2007). CBM assesses the different skills covered in the curriculum by providing equivalent measurements of specific mathematical skills, which make it possible to discern student growth (Deno, 2003). CBM data can compare a student's performance with that of peers and monitor a student's response to instruction or intervention (Wright, 2007). The CBM assessments, or probes, are a series of timed problems in which a student is scored on accuracy of responses. They have the ability to assess multiple competencies (e.g., only double-digit by double-digit multiplication, multi-digit division as well as multiplication). CBMs can be teacher-created, used as worksheets from a variety of sources, or taken from commercial programs that can be found online on sites such as easyCBM (www.easycbm.com), Intervention Central (www.interventioncentral.org), and DIBELS (http://dibels.uoregon.edu). Many common CBM-based programs are used in today's schools.

The first step in CBM is determining the skills students are expected to acquire through the mathematics curriculum. These may be guided by a district curriculum, state curricula, or in most states, the Common Core State Standards. We first identify the learning objectives for students; that is, what they should know and be able to do after completing a lesson, unit, semester, or year of study. In Raphael's case the identified objectives were multi-digit multiplication and division of whole numbers.

STEP 2. SELECT THE MEASUREMENT STRATEGY: HOW DO I KNOW MY STUDENTS ARE LEARNING?

Once we have identified the skills our students will be able to demonstrate after their course of study, the next step is to determine how these skills will be measured. A variety of assessment options are available today, which are usually determined by district and/or building policy. Sometimes teacher-designed assessment tools are also used. But while the choice of measurement tool may already be determined, it is important for teachers to understand the types and varieties of measurement tools that are available in an RTI model. Table 4.3 illustrates the four major types of measurement tools: screening, progress monitoring, diagnostic, and outcome.

Regardless of the tool selected, the key criterion is its ability to yield data to help the teacher determine whether students are learning and, if not, how to target instruction to address specific areas of difficulty. Table 4.4 offers questions to consider when selecting an appropriate measurement tool.

Table 4.3 Comparison of Measurement Tools

Type	Purpose	Description
Screening	Predict student performance	• administered to all students as an initial baseline • quick and efficient measures of overall ability and critical skills • help to identify students who do not meet or who exceed grade-level expectations
Progress monitoring	Determine whether students are making adequate progress	• brief and periodic • data collected, evaluated, and used on an ongoing basis • determine rate of a student's progress • analyze and interpret gaps between benchmarks and achievement • provide information on the effectiveness of instruction and to modify the intervention if necessary
Diagnostic	Provide information for planning more effective instruction and interventions	• provide an in-depth, reliable assessment of targeted skills • may offer new or more reliable information about a student's academic or behavioral needs
Outcome	Give school leaders and teachers feedback about the overall effectiveness of their instructional program	• group-administered tests of important outcomes • given at the end of the school year

Table 4.4 Selecting a Measurement Tool

How will data be collected?	This includes the measurement tools that will be used, the frequency of measurement, and the duration of the assessment. These can be viewed as ground rules so that all those involved in data collection do so with fidelity.
What materials will be used to collect data?	These would include resources needed to record the student's performance, such as student work samples, assessment results, or anecdotal notes by a teacher.
In which settings will data be collected?	In an RTI model, there may be several settings for data collection depending on the tier of intervention the student is in. A student receiving Tier 3 interventions may be seen in multiple settings, and the data collection needs to be defined and complied with to maximize its utility.
Who will be responsible for data collection?	A procedural need, it assigns accountability to those who collect the data, input the data, and organize the data for review and analysis.

Source: Burton & Kappenberg (2012, p. 27).

STEP 3. ESTABLISH A BASELINE: WHERE ARE MY STUDENTS PRESENTLY?

Once we have determined how the students' skills will be measured and progress monitoring assessments selected within the RTI framework, we are then ready to determine a baseline assessment level.

When a teacher has designated a student as requiring closer monitoring and who may receive additional supports (approximately 15%–20% of students, following conventional RTI pyramids), the teacher needs to deter-

> The *baseline assessment* is a student's score before the implementation of an intervention.
> The *baseline assessment score* tells us the student's level of proficiency on the targeted mathematical skill before implementation of an intervention.

mine the student's level of performance and rate of progress, sometimes known as the pre-intervention or the baseline phase of progress monitoring. This requires collecting a set number of scores or data points (usually three to five) that are plotted on a chart (Wright, 2007).

Baseline data also help estimate the student's *rate of improvement* (ROI), which is the average growth or gain between testing intervals. That may be a measurement of how many correct digits the student scores for a math problem or the number of words correctly identified for a reading assignment on probes given at specific intervals of instruction. From these data, the student's growth is calculated and projected given the current rate of growth to create a trend line (National Center on Student Progress Monitoring, n.d.), which estimates the level of performance and proficiency the student is likely to reach at the end of a time interval (e.g., 6 weeks, a marking period, the end of the year) based on current conditions, with no additional intervention.

There are several ways of calculating ROI. For our purposes, we will calculate it by taking the difference between the first and last baseline score and dividing by the number of weeks between them. For example, if Raphael's baseline data are collected weekly for 6 weeks, and his scores are 6, 10, 11, 10, 16, and 18 correct digits respectively on the nine-problem probe, his rate of progress would average 2.0 correct digits per week: the initial score of 6 correct digits, and the final score of 18 correct digits, divided by 6 weeks = 2.0 digits per week. Note that the middle scores do not affect the calculation; all that is considered is the initial and final scores (levels of achievement). At this rate, over a 6-week period, he would be expected to increase by 12.0 digits: a growth rate of 2.0 digits per week times 6 weeks = 12.0 digits. Student progress can be represented on a graph to make the information more accessible for teachers, administrators, and parents. Figure 4.1 illustrates Raphael's actual scores (number of correct digits) and projected rate of improvement (sometimes called the *trend line*).

Figure 4.1   Raphael's Actual Scores and Projected Rate of Improvement

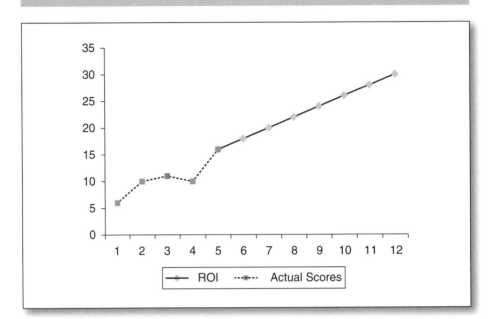

Figure 4.1 shows how the actual ROI on curriculum-based measures can give a clear picture of where a student is in relation to an academic goal, in this case, computing correct digits in a 4-minute activity. Raphael's initial scores for the first 6 weeks are shown. The scores indicate an average growth of 2 correct digits per week. If Ms. Diaz's goal for Rafael was 35 correct digits out of 36 digits after 12 weeks, the ROI would need to be 3 correct digits per week. If the trend line leads to a final level of lower than 36 correct digits after 12 weeks, Ms. Diaz should consider moving Raphael to the next level of RTI, Tier 2.

STEP 4. CREATE A GOAL: WHERE DO MY STUDENTS NEED TO BE?

Once we have determined the student's baseline score, we are then ready to determine a goal. We call this a benchmark assessment score.

The *benchmark assessment score* is the goal the student needs to achieve by the end of the curriculum unit.

For each skill set, the student is expected to attain a *benchmark assessment score* at the completion of the course of study.

Students identified as below benchmark are considered at risk of not mastering the grade-level skills. For groups of students not meeting benchmark, depending on their school's RTI protocol, progress monitoring will be necessary as these students receive instructional supports in addition to the regular classroom instruction. Some schools administer diagnostic assessments to students scoring below a designated number before deciding on an intervention strategy. This additional step can more accurately identify why a student did not achieve benchmark. For example, does the student have the prerequisite skills needed to master the new material?

When we compare the benchmark assessment score with the baseline assessment score from Step 3, two projections can be drawn. The first is the actual ROI if the current conditions continue, sometimes referred to as the *trend line*. The second projection is the anticipated rate of improvement that will be needed to achieve a particular goal, which can be referred to as the *goal line*. When the trend line seriously diverges from the goal line, the RTI framework calls for an appropriate, research-based intervention in an attempt to bring the two lines closer together.

If the trend line leads to a final level that is lower than the goal line, a more intensive instructional approach is indicated. If the trend line leads to a final level that is higher than the goal line, the teacher should consider raising the student's goal to match the probable outcome of the trend. Let's take a look at how Ms. Diaz used these ideas to expand on Raphael's educational program.

Using weekly CBM probes, Ms. Diaz tracked Raphael's progress on a chart that compared his current rate of progress to the CCSS goal for the 12 weeks, which is 35 correct digits out of 36. The six data points showed that, while he was demonstrating some evidence of growth, it was minimal and, on the current trend line, Raphael would not make adequate progress toward the CCSS goal. Figure 4.2 shows Raphael's progress over the first 6 weeks, including (1) the trend line for his projected rate of improvement without intervention and (2) the goal line he would need to follow in order to reach the CCSS goal of 35 by the end of the curriculum unit.

At this point, Ms. Diaz referred Raphael to her building's RTI committee. She presented the Grade 3 spring and Grade 4 fall benchmark data, described her instruction and Tier 1 intervention strategies, and shared Raphael's 12-week progress monitoring data. The committee determined that the goal Ms. Diaz set was, in fact, appropriate, but that Raphael needed a more intensive intervention. At this point, Raphael would move to Tier 2 in the RTI model. His program would continue the Tier 1 support from Ms. Diaz, where growth was demonstrated, and would now include work with Ms. Allen, the math support teacher, in a three-student group for 20 minutes three times a week.

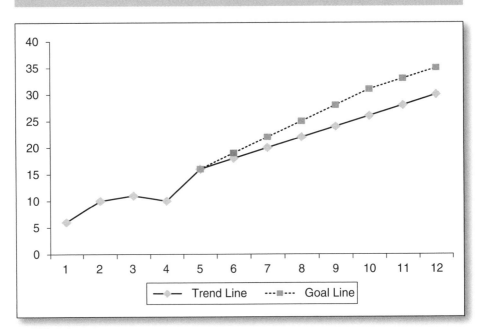

Figure 4.2   Raphael's Trend Line for Projected ROI and Goal Line
Needed to Reach CCSS Goal

In spite of the pressure for students to meet exit criteria, achieve standards, or pass an assessment at the end of the year, the process of goal setting in RTI should not be based on hard-and-fast rules. It needs to consider each student's individual baseline data and rate of improvement as well as curriculum standards, such as the CCSS in mathematics.

Goal setting is always a fluid process in that individual student goals need to be reexamined at set intervals and current rates of progress during intervention phases need to be considered. For example, to continue with Raphael's case, if his ROI increased, it may be appropriate to increase the goal, or shorten the intervention, based on his increased rate of progress. Or we may need to recognize that a goal was too lofty and, based on the rate of progress, lower it.

STEP 5. DEVELOP A CHART OR GRAPH: ARE MY STUDENTS GROWING?

At almost every point in progress monitoring, we rely on graphs to clarify the complex steps of the process. Just as the eyes are the window to the soul, graphs are the window to understanding progress monitoring. While data are essential to understanding how students are progressing in their academic work, raw numbers, even in the form of well-organized tables, can be difficult to comprehend. When the same numbers are presented in charts or graphs, suddenly we seem to understand what the data are telling us

(Wright, 2007). Even the youngest students can immediately see where they are in relation to their goals, what they need to do to improve, and become more involved in doing what they need to in order to get there.

While there are countless ways of presenting data as a chart or graph, the format we have been using in this chapter, a line graph, is among the most commonly used in progress monitoring. In it, time is displayed along the X-axis and the student's test scores are shown on the Y-axis. Since progress monitoring usually calls for brief but frequent probes, it is usually best to plan the graph around weekly, and sometimes daily, time intervals. Planning your graph is important, since it is difficult to reformat a graph from weekly to daily intervals or vice versa once the process has begun.

In the graphs in Figures 4.1 and 4.2, the Y-axes indicate Raphael's level of performance, the scores he received on each probe. It is usually most effective to design the Y-axis so that the student's initial scores fall close to the bottom of the chart and the goal score just below the top. However, be aware that some students may show a decline in results and others may eventually exceed the goal. It may be a good idea to leave some extra margins below the initial scores and above the goal score.

After designing the graph, the next step is to enter the student's initial test scores as points on the graph. When approximately five points are entered, it is possible to introduce two critical elements to the graph: the goal line and the trend line. Several statistical methods, such as regression analysis, can be used to perform these calculations (Hutton, Dubes, & Muir, 1992), but teachers can use the simpler ways presented in this chapter to gain a useful hands-on picture of the path a student needs to follow in reaching an academic goal.

You may recall, the trend line is a straight line drawn between the first and last baseline score and extended to the end of the curriculum unit. The line is drawn so that the slope shows the average expected change in the student's scores, extended to the end of the time period of the graph. This is an approximation of the student's current trend toward improvement. The trend line is used to evaluate whether the student is likely to reach the goal if the current ROI continues.

Also, the goal line shows the path between a student's current level of performance and the goal for the course or activity. It is a straight line, drawn on a graph, between the set of initial scores, at the lower left corner of the graph, and the goal point, at the upper right corner. This is drawn after the first few initial scores, usually within a week of starting a new program. For example, in Raphael's case, this would be a straight line from the 1-week point to the 12-week point (a score of 35; see Figure 4.2).

A simple visual inspection of the trend line and goal line allows the teacher to see if they will converge in the time allotted. If the trend line is consistently below the goal line, the student will most likely not reach the goal without additional interventions.

STEP 6. CREATE A DECISION-MAKING PLAN: HOW DO I GET MY STUDENTS TO WHERE THEY NEED TO BE?

The relationship between the goal line and trend line informs decisions about a student's program in an RTI framework. The following are the three most common scenarios for this relationship.

1. The slope of the trend line is lower than the slope of the goal line (see Figure 4.2).

This is the most common condition. It indicates that unless something changes, the student will not reach the goal. The obvious response is to introduce a change that offers the chance to increase the rate of the student's improvement—called the *intervention* in the RTI process.

2. The slope of the trend line is higher than the slope of the goal line (see Figure 4.3).

Figure 4.3   Slope of Trend Line Is Higher Than Slope of Goal Line

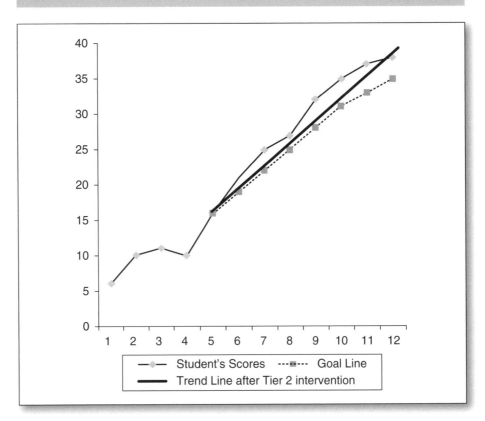

This is an ideal and relatively unusual finding. It indicates that the goal is not challenging enough and should be increased so that the two lines come closer to coinciding.

3. The slopes of the trend line and goal line are generally identical (see Figure 4.4).

In this case, the student can be expected to achieve the goal and no change should be made.

Once these relationships are understood, a teacher or supervisor can transform a mechanical data-gathering process into an insightful and creative decision-making process.

A final point is to keep in mind that "this is not rocket science." It is not a question of whether rocket science is inherently more difficult or complex than teaching children. In fact, most people who understand the two areas agree that it is far more difficult to achieve success with children than with space vehicles: The number and complexity of the variables is enormously greater. The difference is in the need for mathematical precision.

Figure 4.4   Slope of Trend Line and Goal Line Are Generally Identical

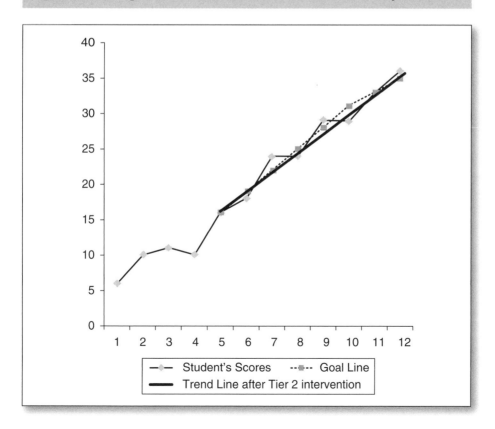

Rocket science depends on the closest attention to the details of mathematical calculation: A number that is accurate to a hundredth place after the decimal point is better than one that is accurate to only a tenth. In working with students, an overemphasis on mathematical precision is not always a good use of time.

The best approach to utilizing data and measurements in progress monitoring is to see data as *indicators* or clues to what is happening and what is needed to improve. A trend line that is drawn a few points off from the exact mathematical calculation can give the same useful information as one that is accurate to a hundredth of a degree.

Using progress monitoring, teachers and supervisors can easily focus on the general trends that become visible by charting the data and make more effective decisions to alter the ones that need improvement.

The 6 weeks spent with Ms. Allen moved Raphael further along in terms of points scored on his weekly probes; however, the trajectory of his trend line was still below the goal line (see Figure 4.5).

Figure 4.5   Raphael's Scores After 6 Weeks of Tier 2 Intervention (Weeks 5–10)

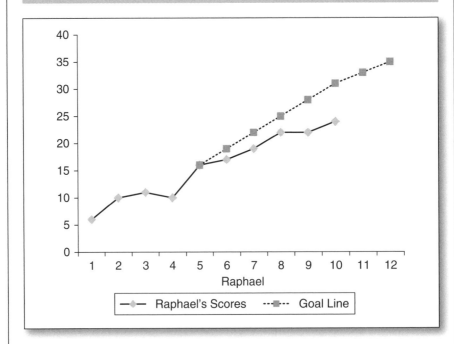

So while Raphael's performance trajectory was closing the gap on his goal line compared to the Tier 1 intervention, it would still fall short of the benchmark goal. Ms. Allen conferred with Ms. Diaz and agreed that more intensive support would be required for Raphael to achieve the goal.

Ms. Diaz and Ms. Allen shared these data with the RTI committee. Raphael had established a rapport with Ms. Allen and looked forward to working with her. "She helps me do better in math," he had commented. The committee determined that Ms. Allen would work individually with Raphael in a Tier 3 intervention. Within this intensive, individualized setting, Ms. Diaz still would work with Raphael daily and share his work with Ms. Allen. At the same time, Raphael would work with Ms. Allen individually four times a week for 20 minutes. Weekly probes would be administered and reviewed again after 6 weeks in Tier 3.

Progress Monitoring Is Ongoing

The initial thought of many teachers new to RTI or progress monitoring is something along the line of, "I have to give *more* tests? I have to collect and track *more* data? I have to do this for *every* student?" In general, the answer is yes. However, the tests used for progress monitoring are different from most of the tests that teachers have given in the past. First, the format, context, and purpose have a single specific focus: to diagnose how well students are learning as a result of the current method of teaching and to try to identify error patterns. These tests are designed to provide information on both how students are learning and how effective the current methods of teaching are. Second, these tests need to be frequent and brief (no more than a few minutes in length), rather than occasional and intensive. When done properly, multiple brief tests can be less time-consuming for teachers than occasional longer tests—and provide much more useful information.

The Outcomes From Progress Monitoring Are Many

- *It gives specific data* on how individual students are progressing toward mastery through the curriculum. We can learn in a period of weeks whether a student is responding positively, negatively, or neutrally to instruction or intervention.
- *It allows us to speak about students' learning* at a level of depth and detail not possible until the widespread integration of progress monitoring and RTI.
- *Teachers learn effective strategies for using data* to address their students' learning challenges and build a repertoire of the most successful of these, which can serve as a resource for them and be shared with their colleagues.

- *Curriculum leaders can analyze trends* in classroom data and determine if there are gaps in the curriculum that need to be addressed.
- *RTI teams can build case studies* as references with respect to which interventions, settings, and frequencies were used with success.
- *Administrators can design professional development* for staff when trends in high student needs surface in certain skill or concept areas.

Prior to starting the Tier 3 individual intervention, Ms. Allen administered another diagnostic math assessment to determine Raphael's greatest deficit areas. She used the results and data from the progress monitoring to select research-based instruction and intervention strategies that matched Raphael's needs and devised a 6-week plan to move him toward his goal.

After 6 weeks of Tier 3 interventions, Raphael's trend line moved even closer to his goal line, for the first time indicating he might actually achieve his goal. After sharing these data with the RTI committee coordinator, Ms. Allen continued working with Raphael during the next 6 weeks with the positive trend continuing. At the spring benchmark assessment, which marked the end of three tiers of intervention, Raphael did indeed meet his goal on the district assessment. The documentation of Raphael's progress and his performance data from the benchmarks and diagnostic assessments would be important in determining what interventions he would receive the following year in the fifth grade.

Progress Monitoring and the Common Core State Standards

As the Common Core State Standards become fully implemented and drive classroom instruction, progress monitoring in the RTI framework should become a more natural and routine activity. The six instructional shifts identified for mathematics (see Table 4.5) promote a more focused and coherent approach toward teaching strategies and concepts.

The transformation presented here can do away with the mile-wide, inch-deep approach in which teachers are required to cover a wide breadth of mathematical topics at a shallow level of understanding, and replace it with a deeper approach to learning fewer topics. This, in turn, can allow teachers to administer assessments with enough frequency and versatility to ensure their students have, in fact, mastered a concept, and when they did not, to still have the appropriate time to reteach the skills and concepts.

In progress monitoring, teachers either design or select assessments tailored to the demands of outcome skills in the Common Core State Standards.

Table 4.5   Common Core Instructional Shifts in Mathematics

Shift 1	**Focus**	Teachers significantly narrow and deepen the scope of how time and energy are spent in the math classroom. They do so in order to focus deeply on only the concepts that are prioritized in the standards.
Shift 2	**Coherence**	Principals and teachers carefully connect the learning within and across grades so that students can build new understanding on foundations built in previous years.
Shift 3	**Fluency**	Students are expected to have speed and accuracy with simple calculations; teachers structure class time and/or homework time for students to memorize, through repetition, core functions.
Shift 4	**Deep understanding**	Students deeply understand and can operate easily within a math concept before moving on. They learn more than the trick to get the answer right. They learn the math.
Shift 5	**Application**	Students are expected to use math and choose the appropriate concept for application even when they are not prompted to do so.
Shift 6	**Dual intensity**	Students are practicing and understanding. There is more than a balance between these two things in the classroom—both are occurring with intensity.

Source: EngageNY.org (2012).

With the detail of the new standards by grade level, strand, and skill set, teachers have the opportunity to create curriculum-based measures that directly address each skill at each level, or they can choose from commercially available Common Core–based assessments.

Schools can either design their own curriculum-based measures or select them from online sources, such as those mentioned earlier (easyCBM, Intervention Central, DIEBELS). Whatever the source, CBMs should cover the concepts of the Common Core State Standards for mathematics in the grade levels to which teachers are assigned. At the same time, teachers should develop assessments that address domains and clusters that reflect the needs of their students. This is a constant process of using CBM to balance the mandates of CCSS with the needs of individual students.

The same process could potentially be applied at all grade levels, and the advantage of progress monitoring is that it will be the same process throughout: identify a standard, select the measurement or assessment, record the data, graph the data, and analyze the results as described earlier. Using progress monitoring as a data gathering and analysis tool in the RTI framework, schools can take full advantage of the Common Core State Standards and move their students toward mastery of their key skills and knowledge.

Tech Byte

INTERVENTION CENTRAL

www.interventioncentral.org/tools/math-worksheet-generator

Jim Wright's RTI-resource website offers educators, at no cost, the ability to generate their own CBM worksheets that are customizable across several mathematics-based skills and concepts. Also on his site is Chart Dog (www .interventioncentral.org/tools/chart_dog_graph_maker), a feature that allows users to enter the parameters and generate time-series graphs. Chart Dog is user-friendly in that teachers or students can enter and save the latest PM data and track progress.

Two core components of progress monitoring are the ability to collect data and to develop a system to monitor the trends within those data. Mathematics lends itself very nicely to the collection of data in that it is readily open to simple right-or-wrong analysis. Curriculum-based measures are a common, efficient, and effective tool in the RTI model, and fortunately for the consumer, resources are widely available for classroom use. Intervention Central offers a variety of free tools useful for progress monitoring in mathematics, including CBMs and graphing or charting.

The site offers CBMs in mathematics, worksheets, and graphing applications (see Figure 4.6).

Within this section of the site, visitors have the ability to customize their own CBM using the worksheet generator, which asks the user to select a mathematics topic, customize the numbers included (e.g., two- or three-digit numbers), and generate a worksheet.

Several sites are linked within Intervention Central's CBM page, including EasyCBM. The Lite Edition offers free registration, and while this has limited options compared to the full version, it includes all that is needed to create CBMs for use in the classroom. Figure 4.7 shows a screenshot from this site.

Users can maintain student groups; select CBM probes from kindergarten through the eighth grade in math numbers and operations, geometry, and algebra; select a written or online assessment; and maintain data using the easyCBM system. Reports can be generated by individual student, student groups, or interventions and are Excel-compatible.

Figure 4.6   Intervention Central Response to Intervention Screenshot

Source: www.interventioncentral.org

Figure 4.7   Intervention Central CBM Options Screenshot

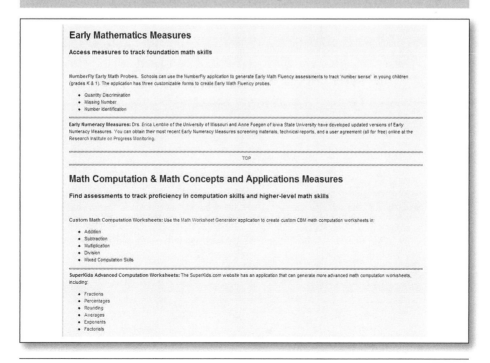

Source: http://www.interventioncentral.org/tools/math-worksheet-generator

Resources for Further Study

CBM Warehouse

www.jimwrightonline.com/htmdocs/interventions/cbmwarehouse.php

A sister website to Jim Wright's Intervention Central, the warehouse contains dozens of links to CBM resources that cover what CBM is, how to do it, where to find it, and a number of sites that allow users to generate their own CBMs.

easyCBM

www.easycbm.com

easyCBM offers its Lite version free of charge and allows visitors to select from premade progress monitoring tools or to create their own through a drop-down menu that includes a range of math topics.

National Center on Response to Intervention

www.rti4success.org

This website includes information on resources, research, and literature; tools and interventions; training and events; and professional development and technical assistance opportunities, as well as links to state-related RTI resources.

National Center on Student Progress Monitoring

www.studentprogress.org

Funded by the U.S. Department of Education, this website includes a resource library, a technical review of PM tools, and general information on the role PM plays in successful schools and data systems.

5 Connecting Mathematics and Literacy

If a Picture Is Worth a Thousand Words, How Many Words Is an Equation Worth?

Dolores Burton and Charlotte Rosenzweig

Mathematical communication is a way of sharing ideas and clarifying understanding. Through communication, ideas become objects of reflection, refinement, discussion, and amendment. When students are challenged to communicate the results of their thinking to others orally or in writing, they learn to be clear, convincing, and precise in their use of mathematical language.

—National Council of Teachers of Mathematics (2000, p. 4)

In this chapter you will learn:

- The importance of teaching students the language of mathematics
- A definition of mathematical literacy
- Seven strategies and activities for promoting mathematical literacy
- Common Core State Standards (CCSS) resources for developing mathematics vocabulary
- Literacy, mathematics, CCSS, and Response to Intervention (RTI) Tiers 1, 2, and 3

Mr. Kirn has been teaching mathematics for 12 years in San Marco School. Over the years he has developed a list of words from the fifth-grade mathematics textbook that, for some of his students, created challenges he believes have interfered with their mastery of mathematical concepts. His students come from diverse backgrounds and experiences. To level the playing field this year, he has decided to focus on teaching literacy as part of the mathematics curriculum driven by the Common Core State Standards. His school has implemented a program of Response to Intervention, so he will begin with identifying the important vocabulary for his Tier 1 instruction on the unit addressing the CCSS for fifth-grade geometry.

The CCSS set high, clear, and consistent expectations for all students. Each student enters the classroom with a different combination of strengths and experiences. The framework of RTI can provide a structure to implement the high benchmarks of the CCSS for all students, address their individual needs, and develop the mathematical literacy that is essential for success in the workforce or higher education.

What Is Mathematical Literacy?

There are many definitions of mathematical literacy, including the ability to interpret equations, understand mathematical representations, and learn the vocabulary used in mathematics textbooks. For our purposes we will use the definition of mathematical literacy created by the National Council of Teachers of Mathematics (NCTM; 2000): "The ability to read, listen, think creatively, and communicate about problem situations, mathematical representations, and the validation of solutions will help students to develop and deepen their understanding of mathematics" (p. 80).

In this chapter we will discuss strategies that may assist struggling students to develop skills in mathematics by facilitating their ability to "read, listen, think creatively, and communicate" about mathematics. We will start with one component of mathematical literacy, the language of mathematics, and examine the challenges some students face with the vocabulary of mathematics.

How Is Math Vocabulary Different From Other Vocabulary?

Many of the students in our classes come to school without the experiences and background knowledge that form the foundation for new learning. As a result, struggling readers may find that reading a mathematics textbook, deciphering words and phrases in word problems, and learning the vocabulary needed to understand mathematics concepts are insurmountable barriers to academic success (Miller, 1993). Instruction in subject-specific vocabulary terms can help to create the background knowledge some students may not possess and is essential for academic success in mathematics.

> Schell (1982) maintained that mathematics texts can contain more concepts per line, sentence, and paragraph than any other kind of texts.

Reading Mathematics Textbooks and Materials

The challenges of reading and understanding textbooks and other mathematics materials are reasons that some students find it difficult to understand mathematical concepts. Mathematical materials are different than those of other content areas. Schell (1982) maintained that mathematics texts can contain more concepts per line, sentence, and paragraph than any other kind of texts. Students also may be confused by the following: (1) multiple words used to describe the same concept (e.g., 5 *times* 2 and 5 *multiplied by* 2), (2) homophones, or words that sound the same but have different spellings and meanings (e.g., *pi* and *pie*), or (3) homonyms or two different words that sound the same and have the same spelling but have multiple meanings (e.g., *measure*). See Table 5.1 for more examples of homonyms used in some textbooks that may cause confusion for students.

A great many domain-specific words in mathematics have other definitions in English when we use them in common situations. One example of a homonym with multiple meanings is the word *degrees*. In common language, *degrees* may be used as a measurement of temperature. In mathematics, *degrees* are used to measure the size of an angle. When a student hears that an angle is 90 degrees, he or she may get confused by thinking that it is a temperature; similarly, when a student hears that the temperature outside is 75 degrees, he or she might be confused and think of it as the degrees of an angle. One strategy a teacher can use when introducing these types of homonyms is to immediately point out any possible areas of confusion, rather

Table 5.1   Some Examples of Homonyms That May Be Confusing

Word	Non-Mathematical Meaning	Mathematical meaning
plane	A machine that is built to fly	A two-dimensional figure
odd	Something different or unusual	An integer that is not a multiple of 2
mean	The act of being unkind	The average of a list of numbers
product	Something you buy	The outcome of a multiplication problem

than assume students understand that the mathematical meaning is different than the meaning in common usage. Anticipate potential misunderstanding, rather than wait for students to make mistakes.

Another example of a homonym is the word *identity*. In common usage, the definition of *identity* would be "that which defines a certain person or thing." In mathematics, the definition of the *identity* property of addition is "the sum of a number and 0 is the number itself." Similarly, the identity property of multiplication is defined as "the product of a number and 1 is the number itself." Examples of the mathematical definitions of *identity* are found in Table 5.2. The teacher can help students see a relationship between the common understanding and mathematical use of the word *identity* by pointing out that—just as the identity of a person or thing never changes—the identity of a number does not change if 0 is added to it or if 1 is multiplied by it.

Table 5.2   The Identity Property of Addition and the Identity Property of Multiplication

Property	*Examples*
Identity property of addition	$19 + 0 = 19, -12 + 0 = -12, a + 0 = a$
Identity property of multiplication	$19 \times 1 = 19, -12 \times 1 = -12, a \times 1 = a$

Homophones—words that sound similar but have different meanings and spellings—may also be confusing because the words have different meanings in mathematics and non-mathematics contexts. Table 5.3 describes some examples of common homophones.

Table 5.3   Common Homophones With Mathematics and Non-Mathematics Definitions

Math Word	*Math Definition*	*Non-Math Word*	*Non-Math Definition*
sum	The result of adding 2 or more quantities	*some*	A few or not all
two	One more than 1	*too*	Also
arc	A portion of the circumference of a circle	*ark*	A large boat

In mathematics instruction, if teachers use charts and graphic organizers to point out differences in word meanings when they are used in specialized contexts and content areas, then students will have a better chance of understanding the specialized vocabulary of different content areas. They can also clear up confusions and misconceptions about word meanings and their applications. More information on this will be presented later in the chapter.

Reading mathematics texts and materials requires special skills, especially for solving word problems and interpreting mathematical signs, symbols, and graphics not used in other content areas. Students also need to read and interpret information presented in unfamiliar ways—not only reading left to right, but also sometimes top to bottom (as in tables) and even diagonally (as in graphs). For example, while numbers are usually read from left to right, determining how to begin to read the left end of a large whole number requires understanding the place value of digits, which increases in base 10 by multiples of 10 from right to left.

To understand written text of mathematics, symbols must have meanings for students. Symbols may be confusing either because they look similar (e.g., the square root and division symbols) or because different representations may be used to describe the same process (e.g., $\bullet$, $*$, and $\times$ for multiplication; $5 \times 3 = 15$ is the same as $5 * 3 = 15$) and the same symbol can mean different things (x can mean a variable or "times"; 5×6).

Making meaning or *deep understanding* can be challenging because the same symbol may have different meanings. For instance, a dash can mean "minus" ($5 - 3 = 2$) or "negative" ($-5 + 3 = -2$). Also, multiple symbols may represent the same concept. For example, multiplication can be represented by $\times$ or $*$ ($6 \times 3 = 18$ is the same as $6 * 3 = 18$). Furthermore, placement or ordering of symbols may affect their meaning, as in order of operations $[5(3x + 3) = 15x + 15; 5(3x) + 3 = 15x + 3]$ (Rubenstein, n.d.).

In this chapter we will discuss seven instructional strategies that may be helpful to teach literacy to students struggling with mathematics concepts that could be helped if they had a more fluent understanding of the language of mathematics. The strategies for promoting mathematical literacy are designed to help teachers meet the Common Core State Standards for Mathematics and to promote greater student engagement and deeper understanding of mathematics. By incorporating several of these strategies throughout the school year, teachers can help their students gain a better grasp of mathematical literacy and reading literacy across the content areas.

What Effective Strategies Can Mathematics Teachers Incorporate to Promote Literacy in Mathematics?

STRATEGY 1: AUTHENTIC PERFORMANCE TASKS

Effective assessment of students' deeper understanding of mathematical concepts involves more than tests and quizzes. Performance tasks assess students' problem-solving skills based on real-world problems and "are not merely exercises requiring discrete facts and skills in isolation" (Wiggins & McTighe, 2005, p. 156). In addition, long-term, multi-staged performance tasks present complex challenges that reflect the issues and problems faced by adults. An example of an authentic performance task designed for Grade 6 gives the students the task of minimizing the costs for shipping bulk quantities of jelly beans. In this activity, students take the real-world role of a packing design specialist who works in the packing department of the CubedJellyBeans .Com Company, and they must design a shipping container or product that is safe and cost-effective to ship cube-shaped jelly beans. Then each student must persuade the president of the company that his or her container design is the best and most cost-effective (adapted from Wiggins & McTighe, 2005).

Literacy activities are integrated into this performance task by asking students to explore possible container shapes that include cones, spheres, cubes, pyramids, cylinders, and prisms, and create a list of related mathematics terms and definitions. This list will be used to create a series of crossword puzzles for the class. Access a template for crossword puzzles from www .ehow.com/how_6292789_design-crossword-puzzle-mathematical-terms .html?ref=Track2&utm_source=ask, and have students create a crossword puzzle with the vocabulary terms. The crossword puzzles can be solved by different students in the class or in groups. This activity addresses CCSS Grade 6 Geometry: *Solve real-world and mathematical problems involving area, surface area, and volume.*

Another authentic interdisciplinary project or performance task that incorporates mathematics, history, and geography for Grade 5 is a project called Marching to Pretoria. This activity addresses CCSS Grade 5: *Perform operations with multi-digit whole numbers and with decimals to hundredths.* A group of nine American students are planning a trip for 2 weeks as part of an international exchange program. The vice principal has asked your class to plan and budget a 14-day tour of South Africa to meet South African students and to help students from both countries develop understandings of each other's country, customs, and culture. Plan your trip so that your groups visit sites that are both urban and rural to develop an appreciation of the beauty and diversity of South Africa.

Students should prepare a written tour itinerary, including an explanation of why each site was selected. Included in the budget are meals, lodging, transportation, and a special event of a 2-day safari for the trip. In addition, students will calculate how much the trip will cost per student, per day. The teacher should provide a list of travel websites where students can find information on the cost of airfare, hotels, tours, and so on. The official website of the South African government (www.gov.za) contains information about the country.

To incorporate mathematical and general vocabulary into this performance task, students must find the definitions and use the following terms in their written report: *budget, expenses, itinerary, currency, credit, transactions, account, savings, remit, invoice, balance, deposit.* They also need to create a glossary of terms and definitions at the end of their report.

This type of high-interest, project-based learning assignment exemplifies the strategies and assessments that can develop students' abilities to apply their academic knowledge to a meaningful real-world challenge. In the Common Core State Standards, teachers can find similar recommendations for an interdisciplinary approach to the teaching of literacy.

STRATEGY 2: COOPERATIVE LEARNING, METACOGNITION, AND VERBAL DISCOURSE IN MATHEMATICS INSTRUCTION

Encouraging students to talk to each other about specific academic content can help them deepen their understanding and learning. Vygotsky (1934/1978) maintained that when students talk and interact with one another they internalize new information more easily. Similarly, Grouws and Cebulla (2000) found that having students work on activities, problems, and assignments in groups, followed by whole-class discussion, can increase students' mathematics achievement. When students think aloud and explain their metacognitive strategies to solve a problem, others in the group can benefit from hearing their peers' thinking and problem-solving processes. A 23-minute video that demonstrates the power of verbal discourse as a Grade 4/5 class solves a complex problem (Common Core Math Lesson 4th/5th Grade) can be found at www.youtube.com/watch?v=DxuMgorzZKs.

A cooperative learning strategy to use in mathematics instruction is *think-pair-share*. Student discussion should include thinking aloud and metacognition as students present and discuss their individual solution methods or summarize key points using think-pair-share. Students have time to *think* about a problem individually, then work in *pairs* to solve the problem, and finally *share* their ideas with the entire class. For example, students may first create definitions and pictures of words independently (see Figure 5.1) and then describe their pictures and definitions to one another; finally, they present the definitions and pictures to the class. (For more information about this technique, see Simon, 2013.) Figure 5.1 is an example of student drawings and definition that addresses the Common Core State Standards for Grade 4.

STRATEGY 3: TEACHING VOCABULARY USING FIVE TYPES OF CONTEXT CLUES

Direct teaching of vocabulary has been advocated for many years, but not all strategies for direct teaching are as effective as others (Irvin, 1990).

Figure 5.1   Student Drawings of Mathematical Terms

CCSS.Math.Content.4.MD.C.6 Measure angles in whole-number degrees using a protractor. Sketch angles of specified measure.

Word or Phrase	Picture	Definition
acute angle	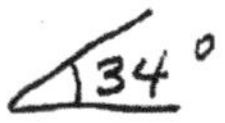 ∠34°	an angle of less than 90°
obtuse angle	 143°	an angle of more than 90°
right angle	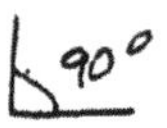 90°	an angle of 90°

Vocabulary can be taught in isolation and alphabetically by previewing vocabulary words and providing students with a list of the new terms that will be covered in a new unit or chapter. However, a much more effective strategy for vocabulary development is to present vocabulary in context, so that the students can see how the unfamiliar words are used correctly in sentences and are connected to important concepts. As a result, the students learn how to figure out the meanings of unknown words (a transferable word building skill) independently. They learn by examining the context clues provided either in the sentence or before/after the sentence that contains the unknown word. Context clues are clues within a sentence or cluster of sentences that reveal the meaning of words. Through explicit instruction, students can be taught how to recognize signal words and contextual clues and then how to use these clues to figure out the meanings of unfamiliar words while reading materials from all content areas. According to Greenwood and Flanigan (2007) this can be a tremendous benefit to students' academic skills, both in expository and mathematical reading.

Five types of context clues can be taught in the mathematics classroom to promote deeper understanding and long-term memory of new terms: *synonym clue, antonym clue, definition clue, punctuation clue,* and *example clue.* Knowing how to use them can enable teachers to create original contextual sentences for teaching new vocabulary terms and, in turn, can help students develop important skills for learning vocabulary and unlocking the meanings of unfamiliar words.

A *synonym clue* is another word in the sentence that is similar in meaning to an unknown word. See the example below.

Synonym Clue Sentence

Five times six is *equivalent* to six times five and is also equal to thirty.

What does the word *equivalent* mean? What is the synonym clue in the sentence?

Answer: Clearly, the synonym clue is "equal to," which is what the word *equivalent* means.

An *antonym clue* is another word in the sentence that is opposite, or in contrast to, the unfamiliar word. See the example below. Please note that a list of antonym signal words has also been provided so teachers can incorporate these signal words into their original antonym clue sentences when designing a math vocabulary lesson.

Antonym Clue Sentence

While finite numbers have definable and measurable limits, time and space are *infinite*.

What does the word *infinite* mean?

What signal word indicates opposites? What is the antonym in this sentence?

Answer: The signal word that indicates opposites is *while*. The antonym in the sentence is *finite*. Thus, the word *infinite* means limitless or having no measurable limits.

Other signal words that indicate contrast are *but, however, although, though, nevertheless, in contrast, even though,* and *rather than.* Teachers of mathematics can incorporate these contrasting signal words into sentences when teaching vocabulary words to help students see contrast between different mathematical terms or concepts (e.g., subtraction vs. addition, dependent variables vs. independent variables, rational numbers vs. irrational numbers).

Definition clues may be signaled by commas or dashes and words or phrases such as *or, that is,* and *in other words.*

Definition Clue Sentence

The *symbol* π is a written mark that represents, or stands for, the quantity that is rounded to 3.14.

What is a symbol?

Answer: In a mathematical context, a symbol is a written mark that stands for a quantity or process. The definition of the expression symbol π is provided directly in the sentence, but students may need help in moving from that specific definition to the more general definition of the word *symbol* itself. They may know that a symbol is something that stands for something else (e.g., a flag represents patriotism), but they need to decipher the precise meaning of the word as it is used in a mathematical context. In this case, the teacher can point out how the specific sentence "The symbol π is a written mark that represents, or stands for, the quantity that is rounded to 3.14" can be transformed to the more universal expression, "A symbol is a written mark that represents, or stands for, something else." Giving students similar sentences to generalize can help develop their skills in using definition clues.

Punctuation Clue Sentence

Punctuation marks can provide clues to a word's meaning.

The *ratio*, or fixed relation in number, of the girls to the boys in the third-grade class is 2:4.

What does the word *ratio* mean? What punctuation clue helped you figure out the meaning of *ratio*?

Answer: Notice that the word is followed by a phrase set off in commas, also known as an appositive phrase (word, definition . . .). Notice that the unknown word is followed by a comma, after which the definition is provided, with another comma following the definition. Instead of the double commas, double dashes and parentheses can also be used as punctuation clues to provide the meaning of unknown words, for example:

- A square—four-sided figure with parallel sides that are equal—is a quadrilateral.
- A square (four-sided figure with parallel sides that are equal) is a quadrilateral.

The definition clue is the easiest type of context clue to find in a sentence; however, struggling learners often benefit from explicit instruction that teaches them how to find these clues.

Example Clue Sentence

Squares, rectangles, and rhombuses are all figures called *quadrilaterals*.

What is a *quadrilateral*? How many sides and angles does a quadrilateral have?

Answer: Since squares, rectangles, and rhombuses are all examples of figures with four sides and angles, students can infer that a *quadrilateral* is a plane figure with four sides and angles.

By teaching students how to use contextual clues to figure out the meanings of new mathematical terms, math teachers are empowering students to think independently and to apply this transferable skill when reading varied materials across content areas.

STRATEGY 4: USE OF GRAPHIC ORGANIZERS

The more knowledge students bring to the classroom, the better they will grasp and understand the new information. Webbing is an effective tool to activate students' prior knowledge. For example, in a class that is learning about polygons, the teacher can start by writing the topic on the board and asking the students to brainstorm by mentioning anything that comes to their minds about the topic. As the students brainstorm, the teacher draws a web with all their ideas, depicting how all these ideas relate to polygons. Making a mental note of the collective prior knowledge and any misinformation or confusion of vocabulary terms demonstrated by the class, the teacher can use this formative assessment to guide the direction of this lesson and of subsequent instruction. Especially important, the teacher needs to openly and explicitly address any homonyms or multiple word meanings that may have been identified during the brainstorming session. Figure 5.2 is an example of a graphic

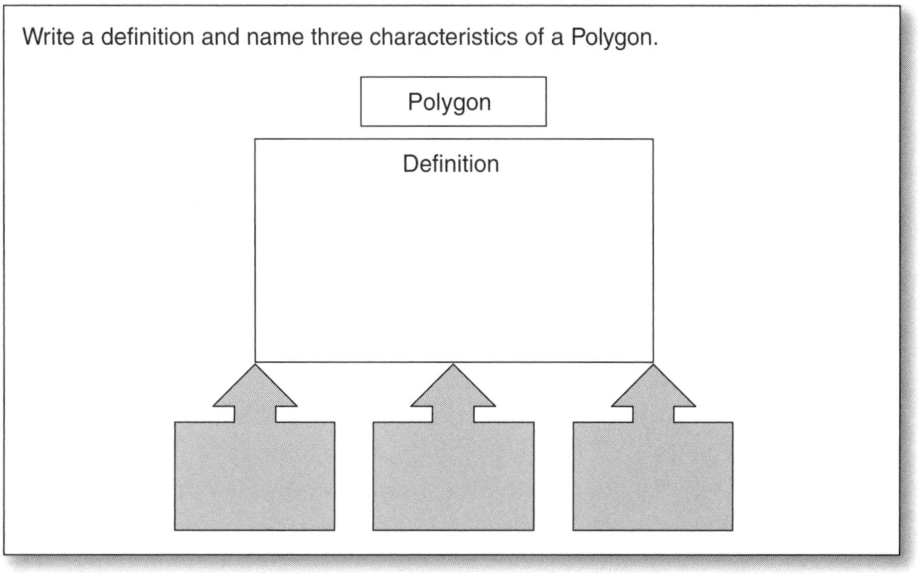

Figure 5.2   Sample Graphic Organizer for Mathematical Terms

organizer for the term *polygon*. The three arrows on the bottom can be used for identifying characteristics, examples, or non-examples.

Kester Phillips, Bardsley, Bach, and Gibb-Brown (2009) have identified other strategies to integrate mathematics and literacy. In addition to graphic organizers used in webbing, some effective strategies include (1) using word roots and prefixes to determine unknown words, (2) giving students opportunities to practice skills interactively in small groups, and (3) creating a word wall of mathematics terms in the classroom.

STRATEGY 5: GAMES, MAGIC SQUARES, AND PUZZLES

One of the goals of mathematics teachers is to engage and motivate a diverse population of students by providing various interesting and purposeful activities that promote critical thinking, problem-solving skills, and deep understanding of mathematical concepts. Manual and online games are intrinsically motivating for students, and teachers can incorporate these entertaining and high-interest activities into their lessons to teach mathematical vocabulary and concepts.

One game that reinforces mathematical and academic vocabulary is a teacher-created cooperative learning activity called Talk a Mile a Minute (Marzano & Pickering, 2005). The teacher divides the class into four teams, and each team selects a "talker" who tries to get his or her team members to say each of the words on the team's list. The talker is allowed to say anything about the terms but may not use any words in the category title or any rhyming words. The first team to gets its players to say all the words on the team list is the winning team. See Table 5.4 for a sample of a completed game activity sheet and directions the teacher can read to the class.

Another game that can be played to reinforce mathematical terms and concepts is called the Synonym-Antonym or Similar-Opposite Game. Students are given a list of mathematical terms and must find either the antonyms or synonyms of the given words. This game can be played as a small-group, paired, or individual activity. The first team to get 10 synonyms or 10 antonyms for the words listed wins. See Table 5.5 for a sample activity sheet. Please note that a challenging independent practice activity to differentiate instruction is also provided. This prompts the students to apply what they learned by searching through their textbook chapters for more words, creating their own synonym or antonym game list, and then exchanging lists with a partner to answer each other's word games. Table 5.6 is a sample activity sheet.

By requiring students to find synonyms and/or antonyms for math terms, teachers are helping students compare and contrast and are simultaneously

Table 5.4 Sample of a Completed Game Activity Sheet

Team 1	*Team 2*
Types of Quadrilaterals	**Two-Dimensional Geometric Shapes**
square	circle
rectangle	square
rhombus	triangle
trapezoid	rectangle
rhomboid	hexagon
trapezium	pentagon
Team 3	*Team 4*
Three-Dimensional Shapes	**Verbs Related to Mathematics**
cone	compute
sphere	multiply
cylinder	estimate
cube	generate
prism	subtract
pyramid	combine

Directions: The class will be divided into four teams. Each team will select a talker who will try to get the team to say each of the words on the team's list. The talker is allowed to say anything about the terms but may NOT use any words listed in the category title or any rhyming words. For example, for the word *square* under the category of Types of Quadrilaterals, the talker can say, "This is a figure with four equal sides and angles."

helping them expand their vocabulary development through word connections and associations.

Magic Squares is a brain-teasing activity that has captured the minds of many children and adults. Why not bring this type of activity into the math class to teach mathematics terms? Teachers design activities with 3×3 or 4×4 matrixes and require students to match the meanings of math terms with their numbered definitions. Students then place the numbers into the boxes so that adding across every row and every column produces a "magic number." See Tables 5.7, 5.8, 5.9, and 5.10 for samples. Note the words used in this Magic Squares activity have been taken directly from the Common Core State Standards for Mathematics for Grades K–8.

Magic Squares Directions: Match the nine words listed in Square A (Table 5.7) with the correct definitions found in Column B (Table 5.8).

Table 5.5   Sample Activity Sheet for the Synonym-Antonym Game

Word	*Antonym (Opposite)*
1. addition	
2. division	
3. finite	
4. overlapping	
5. compose	
6. numerator	
7. horizontal	
8. dependent variable	
9. rational number	
10. symmetrical	

Word Power Challenging Independent Practice Activity Directions: Using your mathematics textbook, make up your own synonym or antonym matching game. Exchange lists with a partner and see who finishes first with the best accuracy.

Then place the numbers into the Magic Squares so that all the numbers in every row and column add up to the same magic number. What is the magic number?

Fill in the numbers in the blank boxes below (Table 5.9) by matching the words in Square A to the appropriate definitions listed in Column B. The first one is done for you. Note that *quotient* means "the result when one number is divided by another number," so the number 4 is placed into the corresponding or matching box, as shown in Table 5.9.

There are many other magic squares that can be used and found online to create fun activities that reinforce and review mathematical terms.

STRATEGY 6: ORAL READING OF CHILDREN'S BOOKS

Oral reading is an authentic reading task that is a vital component of literacy in English classes. It is also an important literacy strategy used in

Table 5.6 Sample Activity Sheet for the Challenging Synonym-Antonym Game

Word	Synonym (Similar Meaning)
1.	
2.	
3.	
4.	
5.	
6.	
7.	
8.	
9.	
10.	

Table 5.7 Magic Square Activity Square A

quotient	numerator	product
multiple	fraction	sequence
numeral	estimate	denominator

Table 5.8   Magic Square Activity Column B (Definitions)

Column B (Definitions)
1. to calculate an approximate value
2. the result when one number is multiplied by another number
3. a number that is a product of a specified number and another number
4. the result when one number is divided by another number
5. any quantity expressed in terms of a numerator and denominator
6. the term below or to the right of the line in a fraction
7. an ordered set of quantities or elements
8. a letter or word expressing a number
9. the term above or to the left of the line in a fraction

Table 5.9   Magic Square Activity

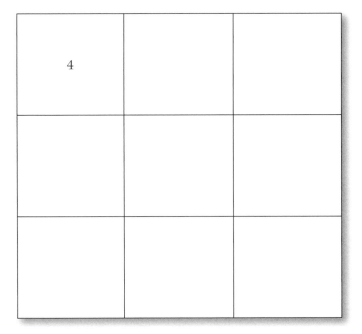

elementary and middle school mathematics classes to promote deeper understanding of specialized mathematics vocabulary and concepts. Research into science, mathematics, and technology instruction has

Table 5.10   Magic Square Activity Answers

4	9	2
3	5	7
8	1	6

The magic number is 15. Horizontally $4 + 9 + 2 = 15$, $3 + 5 + 7 = 15$, $8 + 1 + 6 = 15$, and vertically $4 + 3 + 8 = 15$, $9 + 5 + 1 = 15$, $2 + 7 + 6 = 15$.

shown that frequent oral and written interactions between teachers and students—and among students—including discussions and open-ended follow-up questions, are powerful factors in developing mathematical thinking (Carr & Harris, 2001). Teacher read-aloud activities can include prereading, during reading, and postreading questions and activities, as well as thought-provoking and open-ended questions that involve students in active discussions and promote both teacher-student and student-student interaction.

The following are examples of trade books that can enrich the students' understanding of mathematics vocabulary and concepts, while adding the element of fun to oral reading in math lessons:

• *Sir Cumference and the Dragon of Pi,* by Cindy Neuschwander (1999), brings students into a math adventure in which the main character, Sir Cumference (a clever play on the word *circumference*), is transformed into a fire-eating dragon. Another character, Radius, goes on a quest through a castle to solve a riddle that will reveal the cure for Sir Cumference. Readers must discover a magic number, known as Pi, which is the same for all circles. For many students the concept of Pi (or π) is confusing and complicated.

Students can memorize the formula for the area of a circle ($A = \pi r^2$) or "area of a circle equals pi times r-squared," but do they truly understand the concept of a constant like π? This trade book contains selected vocabulary and concepts of mathematics, combined with eye-catching pictures and a clever, narrative tale, which make the difficult math vocabulary words come alive. As a result, these words and concepts become clearer and more memorable for both upper elementary and middle school students. (CCSS Grade 7: *Know the formulas for the area and circumference of a circle and solve problems; give an informal derivation of the relationship between the circumference and area of a circle.*)

• *Math Doesn't Suck: How to Survive Middle School Math,* by Danica McKellar (2007), is a book designed for middle school girls to heighten their interest in mathematics. The chapters have catchy names and the mathematics concepts are taught through real-world situations. For example, Chapter 1 is titled "How to Make a Killing on eBay." This chapter teaches students the concepts of prime numbers and factoring by placing students into an authentic situation in which they are creating friendship bracelets and grouping beads by numbers and colors. Chapter 4, titled "Everything You Ever Wanted to Know About Pizza but Were Afraid to Ask," uses pizzas to teach students the concepts of fractions and mixed numbers. Teachers can use a text like this to reinforce mathematical concepts by reading—or having students read—relevant chapters aloud. (CCSS Grade 7 Ratios and Proportional Relationships: *Analyze proportional relationships and use them to solve real-world and mathematical problems*; The Number System: *Apply and extend previous understandings of operations with fractions to add, subtract, multiply, and divide rational numbers.*)

• *Comic Strip Math: 40 Reproducible Cartoons With Dozens of Funny Story Problems That Build Essential Skills,* by Dan Greenberg (1998), is a Scholastic high-interest book for Grades 3–6. It uses a special kind of comic strip designed to bring fun and laughter into the mathematics class while teaching serious mathematical concepts and topics specified by the NCTM in context. Greenberg uses comical characters (such as Moovis and Woovis), attractive cartoons, and a whimsical point of view to engage readers in learning mathematics. The book begins with Section 1: Addition, Subtraction, and Place Value, which includes catchy chapter titles such as "You Don't Say," "Doggy Dinner," and "Phoney Baloney." Further on in the book, Section 7: Rate, Ratio, Percent, includes chapter titles such as "Snoozer," "Pulsations," "Hums," and "Family Reunion Picnic." The clever chapter titles, as well as the cartoons and nontraditional presentation of math information, heighten students' interest and motivation to learn mathematical concepts. Greenberg's book can a useful element in effective teaching that develops students' mathematical skills in the context of authentic learning situations. (CCSS Grade 6, four critical areas: [1] *connecting ratio and rate to whole number multiplication and division and using concepts of ratio and rate to solve problems*; [2] *completing understanding of division of fractions and extending the notion of number to the system of rational numbers, which includes negative numbers*; [3] *writing, interpreting, and using expressions and equations*; and [4] *developing understanding of statistical thinking*.)

STRATEGY 7: STRATEGIES FOR DIRECT INSTRUCTION IN MATHEMATICS VOCABULARY

Marzano (2004) has identified a six-step process for direct instruction in content vocabulary:

1. The teacher provides a description, explanation, or example of an unfamiliar vocabulary term.

2. Students construct their own description, explanation, or example of the new term.

3. Students are asked to draw a nonlinguistic representation, such as a picture, symbol, or graphic of the unknown term.

4. Students participate in vocabulary notebook activities designed to provide more knowledge of the word.

5. Students discuss the new word with their peers.

6. Students participate in games (e.g., hangman, crossword puzzles) that reinforce the meaning of the new term.

Table 4.11 describes this process. Teachers may need to provide some models of nonlinguistic representations of words to help students understand how to visually represent certain words using a picture, a graph, or a symbol. For example, teachers may hand out cards that they have prepared with some math words and their representations by teacher-created symbols.

Some other strategies to encourage student discourse include having students describe their pictures and definitions to one another, present examples and non-examples (see Tech Byte later in the chapter), and discuss differences in each other's definitions. For some students, a more hands-on approach is effective, such as having them create a song, poem, poster, or skit describing their word. The vocabulary terms for a mathematics unit can be

Table 5.11   Six-Step Process for Teaching Mathematical Vocabulary

	The Teacher	*The Student*
Step 1	Provides a description, explanation, or example of the new vocabulary and distributes the unit vocabulary list. Prepares 3×5 cards with one word on each and places them face down for students to choose.	Choses which vocabulary word to define by picking a card from the pile of cards containing vocabulary words for the unit.
Step 2	Provides a Frayer Model graphic organizer to help students identify important facts in their definition. Demonstrates using a graphic organizer to describe one vocabulary word.	Uses the graphic organizer to construct his or her own description, explanation, or example of the word.
Step 3	Provides an example of a picture or other nonlinguistic representation of the word. For example, draws a picture of a tree whose branches contain different kinds of angles and labels them.	Draws a nonlinguistic representation, such as a picture, symbol, or graphic of his or her word.
Step 4	Finds a picture of each kind of angle represented in a real-world object and discusses it with the students. What are the similarities, characteristics, etc.?	Finds picture of each kind of angle represented in a real-world object and chooses one to add to the graphic organizer.
Step 5	Divides the class into groups and provides a structure for the discussion, assigning roles for members of each group, including recorder and reporter. Provides materials for a student-created dictionary or children's book demonstrating pictures and definitions of the different kinds of angles.	Discusses the vocabulary word with peers in the group and refines his or her own definitions. Finalized definitions are reported to the whole group. A group dictionary is created and shared with the class.
Step 6	Distributes a choice of three games: 1. Pictionary—students have paper and draw a picture to convey the meaning of the word. 2. Angle search—the teacher provides a picture and students identify angles in the picture. 3. Crossword puzzle—students solve a teacher-made crossword puzzle or make an original puzzle based on mathematics vocabulary.	Participates in two of the three games.

Source: Marzano & Simms (2013).

divided among groups in the class so that students collectively create their songs or skits. In addition, the relevant academic vocabulary can be presented as a bulletin board display, by enlisting the collaboration of an art teacher, or as an art project. The teaching of the mathematics vocabulary for each unit should precede and then be integrated into the ongoing teaching of the mathematics concepts.

The following section presents an example of a lesson appropriate to each tier, addressing both RTI and the same Common Core State Standard.

Tier 1 Lesson

Common Core State Standard Grade 5: *Understand that attributes belonging to a category of two-dimensional figures also belong to all subcategories of that category. For example, all rectangles have four right angles and squares are rectangles, so all squares have four right angles.*

Research has identified peer-to-peer student discussion as an effective way to help students to comprehend information and gain a deeper understanding that helps to move the information from short-term to long-term memory (Marzano, 2004). For this Tier 1 lesson on the interior angles of a polygon, the teacher might prepare a four-column table, with the number of rows corresponding to the number of unfamiliar vocabulary terms in the lesson. A lesson on polygons might include six unfamiliar words and terms: *angle, right angle, interior angle, exterior angle, obtuse angle,* and *acute angle.* In Table 5.12, each cell of the table contains a new word in Column 1, definitions in Column 2, and attributes in Column 4. The class is divided into groups of four students, and each group is required to write a definition for the word in Column 3, after searching for the definition in at least two sources using their textbook or online resources (such as www.amathsdictionary forkids.com). The teacher then assigns roles. Each group has a designated

- *reader* to read aloud the word and the two definitions that have been identified by the group investigator,
- *investigator* to find the definitions,
- *recorder* to write the definitions with their sources on the table, and
- *reporter* to report to the class when the teacher asks a question about the group's chart results.

The group should discuss the two definitions identified and decide on the definition they wish to use and why. This cooperative learning activity can be followed by students exploring the angles and sides of the polygons on a prepared worksheet and recording any patterns and similarities they find. A short probe to check for mastery is recommended.

Table 5.12   Table of Words, Pictures, Definitions, and Attributes

Word	Actual Definition	Student Definition	Attributes
angle			
right angle			
interior angle			
exterior angle			
obtuse angle			
acute angle			

If, after a designated period of progress monitoring, some students do not reach mastery, Tier 2 interventions should start. In Tier 2, students are given additional time on task, different instructional materials, research-based strategies, and a smaller teacher-to-student ratio. For our Tier 2 intervention, we will provide an additional half hour of instruction twice a week in a small group of four to six students who have not mastered the concepts with Tier 1 instruction.

Tier 2 Lesson

Common Core State Standard Grade 5: *Understand that attributes belonging to a category of two-dimensional figures also belong to all subcategories of that category. For example, all rectangles have four right angles and squares are rectangles, so all squares have four right angles.*

For our Tier 2 lesson we will use the Verbal and Visual Word Association (VVWA) graphic organizer (Eeds & Cockrum, 1985), which is designed to help students understand mathematical vocabulary through visual and personal associations with a particular word. Research shows that this graphic organizer is especially effective with low-achieving and second language learners in content area classes. It enables second language learners and others to make a personal association that can more easily link to their background knowledge.

In Chapter 3 we discussed the importance of this affective domain to learning. The VVWA graphic organizer can help students identify and create a visual reference for unfamiliar concepts and vocabulary. In this Tier 2 activity, students can collect vocabulary graphic organizers for each word in a unit and place them in a loose leaf binder to use for reference as they might use a glossary or dictionary. This can be done as a collaborative project by pairing students. Also, teachers can use vocabulary graphic organizers as assessment for data to guide reteaching or to plan the next step in instruction. Table 5.13 is an example of VVWA graphic organizer. To start, the teacher should create a vocabulary list for the unit. In this case we will use the vocabulary to understand the concepts needed to master the fifth-grade Common Core State Standard on two-dimensional figures as we did in the Tier 1 lesson.

The teacher should then give the following directions:

1. Select the vocabulary term from our polygon vocabulary list.
2. Write the word in the upper left box. Write the definition or description in the lower left box.
3. Draw a visual representation of the word in the upper right box.
4. In the lower right box, describe a personal association (something the students recall from their own experience).

Table 5.13   Verbal and Visual Word Association Graphic Organizer

Word	Visual Representation
Definition	**Personal Association or Characteristic**

To differentiate instruction, teachers can fill in one or more boxes and have students complete the rest of the organizer. The word would be placed on the front of the card and the completed organizer on the back. When students become stuck on a word as they read the text or other materials, they can turn the card over. Completed organizers can also be used on the word wall. Students who continue to struggle after applying the strategy for the designated period of time should be moved to Tier 3. In Tier 3 students receive intensive instructional time on task, different materials, smaller teacher-to-student ratio, and different research-based strategies. For our Tier 3 intervention, we will provide an additional 20 minutes of instruction five times a week in a small group of two to three students who have not mastered the concepts with Tier 2 instruction.

Tier 3 Lesson

Common Core State Standard Grade 5: *Understand that attributes belonging to a category of two-dimensional figures also belong to all subcategories of that category. For example, all rectangles have four right angles and squares are rectangles, so all squares have four right angles.*

For this lesson, we use an adaption of the six-step process identified by Marzano (2004) to address the vocabulary required by the standard. To begin, as with the Tier 1 and Tier 2 lessons, the teacher should examine the textbook chapter on these topics to identify vocabulary that may be problematic for these particular Tier 3 students.

STEP 1: TEACHER PROVIDES A DESCRIPTION, EXPLANATION, OR EXAMPLE OF THE NEW TERM.

For this step the teacher should use a conversational tone, including the sematic features identified by Marzano (2004), not simply read the definition to the students. Focusing on semantic features can help students retain information on content vocabulary. A semantic feature is a device for collecting certain key words of a text into a group, called a *vocabulary megacluster* (Marzano, 2004), that has similar properties or meaning among all the terms. For example, a semantic feature built around the vocabulary megacluster *shapes, direction, position of geometric figures* would include vocabulary words such as *square* (i.e., shape), *adjacent* (i.e., a direction), and *opposite* (i.e., a position). The sematic features relevant to mathematics identified by Marzano are described in Table 5.14.

Table 5.14   Features Relevant to Mathematics Terms

Category	*Semantic Features*
Shapes, direction, position	• Shapes, direction, position has distinguishing features. • Shapes, direction, position is associated with a specific function. • Shapes, direction, position is associated with specific reference points.
Quantities, amounts, measurements	• The quantity, amount, or measurement has a specific relationship with other quantities, amounts, or measurement. • The quantity, amount, or measurement has a specific referent.

Source: Marzano & Simms (2013).

STEP 2: STUDENTS RESTATE THE EXPLANATION OF THE NEW TERM IN THEIR OWN WORDS.

In our example, the students use the graphic organizer to construct their own description, explanation, or example of their word. In this case we suggested the Frayer Model, but there are many others graphic organizers that can be used. Some can be found at www.teachervision.fen.com/math/graphic-organizers/53511.html.

STEP 3: STUDENTS DRAW A NONLINGUISTIC REPRESENTATION OF THEIR WORD, SUCH AS A PICTURE, SYMBOL, OR GRAPHIC.

In this case students would draw one of the angles in the identified list of terms.

STEP 4: STUDENTS DO ACTIVITIES TO ADD TO THEIR KNOWLEDGE OF THE TERM.

In our example, students found real-world pictures of angles. This could include pictures from magazine that the students cut out and paste on a poster. They could also identify different angles in objects in their home and, if available, take a picture with a digital camera and create an electronic compendium of examples of each angle they found.

STEP 5: STUDENTS DISCUSS TERMS WITH ONE ANOTHER.

Students discuss the vocabulary word with others in the group and refine their own definitions. Final definitions are reported and a group dictionary is created and shared with the class.

STEP 6: STUDENTS PLAY GAMES WITH TERMS.

We recommend that teachers give students an opportunity to play games with the vocabulary terms, such as crossword puzzles and Magic Squares, described earlier in the chapter. Other choices may be Hangman, Jeopardy, or Word Finds. Additional games can be found at www.myvocabulary.com.

If at the end of the six-step process, students are still struggling, it may be appropriate to refer them for additional testing by a trained professional with expertise in identifying students with special needs.

This chapter was designed to give teachers strategies to help students understand the vocabulary of mathematics, which is a prerequisite to understanding the content of mathematics. The focus of this chapter was on Mathematical Practices 6:

> Attend to precision. Mathematically proficient students try to communicate precisely to others. They try to use clear definitions in discussion with others and in their own reasoning. They state the meaning of the symbols they choose, including using the equal sign consistently and appropriately. (Council of Chief State School Officers, 2010, p. 7)

We believe that mastering the language of mathematics is essential to helping students master the other skills of mathematics.

In addition to the classroom strategies discussed in this chapter, new mobile devices hold great promise to help students master math vocabulary. For example, a free app for Hangman is available for the iPhone, iPad, iPad Mini, and iPod Touch. Students can use these devices to interact with their mathematics vocabulary anywhere and anytime. The following section contains additional technology that teachers can use to enhance their instruction in the vocabulary of mathematics.

 Tech Byte

WORKSHEET WORKS

www.worksheetworks.com

This website creates custom graphic organizers for use in schools. The Frayer Model is found at www.worksheetworks.com/miscellanea/graphic-organizers/frayer.html.

The Frayer Model (Frayer, Frederick, & Klausmeier, 1969) is a graphic organizer to help students build vocabulary. We will be using this to specifically address the CCSS mathematics vocabulary. The model requires students to (1) define the target vocabulary words or concepts and (2) apply this information by generating examples and non-examples and place the information on a chart that is divided into four sections for visual representation.

To begin, show and explain the Frayer Model diagram to students. Next, prepare a filled-in diagram, using one of the vocabulary words identified for the unit of study. Using whole-class discussion, model how to fill out the diagram. Assign vocabulary words to groups of students and provide a Frayer Model graphic organizer (see Figure 5.3) with each assigned vocabulary word in the middle oval. Give students time to practice with assigned vocabulary in groups. When all groups have completed their Frayer Model for their word, let each group share their work with the class. Display students' diagrams as posters throughout the unit so they can refer to the words and continue to add ideas.

Figure 5.3   The Frayer Model Graphic Organizer

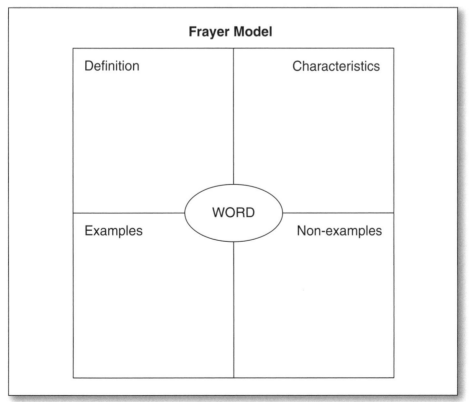

Source: Frayer, Frederick, & Klausmeier (1969). Reprinted with permission.

Resources for Further Study

Mathwords

www.mathwords.com

Written by a teacher, this website is a resource for math vocabulary. It contains formulas and definitions from beginning algebra to calculus. The definitions are student friendly, and the site contains illustrations and examples of the vocabulary words. The alphabet on the left side of the screen accesses math words starting with each letter.

A Maths Dictionary for Kids

www.amathsdictionaryforkids.com

This is an animated, interactive online math dictionary for students. The definitions of over 600 common mathematical terms are described using illustrations and, in some cases, animation.

Granite School District Math Vocabulary

www.graniteschools.org/depart/teachinglearning/curriculuminstruction/math/Pages/MathematicsVocabulary.aspx

This Granite School District (in Salt Lake City, Utah) site contains lists of words by grade level, without definitions. Some of the lists are labeled as CCSS Vocabulary Words by grade level. It also contains links for Dual Immersion, Presentation Materials, Templates, and Activities and Lessons.

Primary Education Oasis

www.primary-education-oasis.com/math-vocabulary-words.html

This site has vocabulary words from the CCSS for mathematics for kindergarten through fifth grade with pictorial definitions and other resources for teaching vocabulary.

Vocabulary Spelling City

www.spellingcity.com/math-vocabulary.html

This site contains lists of vocabulary words in mathematics by grade level. By clicking on a word, students can listen to an audio representation of the word, spelling, and definition. Vocabulary games are available both for free and with a membership to the site.

Math Is Fun: Illustrated Mathematics Dictionary

www.mathsisfun.com/definitions/index.html

This website contains an alphabetical list of definitions of mathematics terms with illustrations and links to further reading. Some of the definitions are animated.

How to Design a Crossword Puzzle With Mathematical Terms

www.ehow.com/how_6292789_design-crossword-puzzle-mathematical-terms.html#ixzz2AdlLe4RT

This article describes several websites that have electronic templates for crossword puzzles. Teachers can use mathematical vocabulary words and definitions to create crossword puzzles.

Wordle

www.wordle.net

This is a free web application that allows students and teachers to create a word cloud based on the frequency of words in a text. To create a word cloud, you paste text into the applet and then manipulate the visual display by selecting the color scheme, layout, and font. Word clouds can be used to highlight words and themes. This application can be used in any content area.

6

English Language Learners

Dolores Burton and Andrea Honigsfeld

Students who speak a first language other than English or have related cultural differences must not face special barriers to learning mathematics. Every student's cultural heritage should be accepted and celebrated for the diversity that it brings to the learning environment. Expanded opportunities should be available to English language learners (ELL students) who need them to develop mathematical understanding and proficiency. Mathematics teachers should have knowledge of content and pedagogy that support ELL students, including an understanding of the role of the first language.

—National Council of Teachers of
Mathematics (NCTM; 2008b, para. 1)

In this chapter you will learn:

- How to overcome barriers to learning for this population
- The difference between the acquisition of social language and the academic language necessary to succeed in mathematics
- Strategies to teach mathematics to ELLs guided by the Common Core in each tier of Response to Intervention (RTI)
- Examples of differences in mathematics teaching and learning between different cultures

Oksana, born in the Ukraine, has been in the United States for more than a year. Her family lives in a new development in town, and her parents speak very little English. Like her three younger siblings, she has made friends, but tends to interact only when approached. While her English skills are improving and her hard work is evident, she experiences a great deal of frustration in the mathematics classroom. In the past, the teacher would ask Oksana to solve problems and give the answer; Oksana would also be told exactly how to arrive at the solution. Now, to succeed, Oksana not only has to provide the right answer, but she has to explain her reasoning and the process she used to arrive at her solution. To make matters worse, she has to do so in English, which she is just acquiring. Oksana is sometimes confused, sometimes frustrated, but always challenged by this new classroom norm that requires sophistication on both mathematical and linguistic levels (Slavit & Ernst-Slavit, 2007).

How can a classroom teacher help Oksana?

Teachers are challenged to create effective learning environments for all students in their classrooms. In the United States, data from the 2000 Census indicate that school districts throughout the country are serving a growing student population whose home languages and cultures are increasing in diversity (47 million individuals). For the 1993–1994 school year, the National Clearinghouse for English Language Acquisition reported a national ELL enrollment of 3,552,497; 10 years later, there were 4,999,481 school-aged ELLs in the United States, reflecting approximately 10.3% of the student body (Slavit & Ernst-Slavit, 2007). "In 2009, some 21 percent of children ages 5–17 (or 11.2 million) spoke a language other than English at home, and 5 percent (or 2.7 million) spoke English with difficulty. Seventy-three percent of those who spoke English with difficulty spoke Spanish" (Aud et al., 2011, para. 1). Nationally, the most populous minority group remains Hispanics, who numbered 52 million in 2011; they also were the fastest growing, with their population increasing by 3.1% since 2010. This boosted the Hispanic share of the nation's total population to 16.7% in 2011, up from 16.3% in 2010 (U.S. Census Bureau, 2012).

Growing evidence suggests that low performance on standardized assessments by some ELLs has little to do with innate mathematical ability and much to do with cultural differences in the ways mathematical concepts are taught in other countries as well as challenges from the vocabulary of mathematics (Richardson & Wilkinson, 2005). Also, sometimes instruction is not geared to grade-level standards and standardized assessments are not in sync with the instruction of this population (Short & Echevarria, 2004/2005).

ELLs may speak social language well—this is usually mastered in 1 or 2 years—but continue to struggle with academic language, which is necessary for success in the content subjects and takes 5 to 7 years to master (Cummins, 2005).

Differences between social language and academic language have been identified by Ernst-Slavit and Slavit's (2007) four *vocabulary types* that are commonly used in mathematics classrooms: high-frequency vocabulary, general vocabulary, specialized vocabulary, and technical vocabulary. Reviewing lessons to identify the type of vocabulary necessary for the concepts to be taught can be helpful to the ELL. The following list describes each type of vocabulary.

- *High-frequency vocabulary* includes words used regularly in everyday conversations (e.g., *small, orange, clock*).
- *General vocabulary* includes words that are not directly associated with a specific content area (e.g., *combine, describe, consequently*).
- *Specialized vocabulary* includes words that one would find in a textbook or conversation within a content area (e.g., *divisor, least common denominator*).
- *Technical vocabulary* includes words specific to a content area topic (e.g., *Pythagorean theorem, integrals, ratio*).

Words that are challenging for some ELLs typically found in mathematics textbooks describe quantitative relationships (e.g., *next, last, most, less, longer*) or logical relationships (e.g., *different from, opposite of, greater than, less than, always, never*). Some of these words or phrases are used in other content areas, as well as in everyday conversation, where the meaning may be different, which makes it even more challenging for ELLs to use these words mathematically. Teachers can help students develop their mathematics vocabulary by integrating some easy-to-follow strategies into their lesson planning using the three-tier RTI framework guided by the Common Core State Standards. Later in this chapter we will explore some of those strategies.

Mastering academic English involves more than vocabulary development; other elements of content-based literacy are needed as well (Short & Echevarria, 2004/2005). Teachers must make sure their students engage in conversations centered around mathematics and use the mathematical vocabulary in sentences. They also need to develop discourse-level comprehension of mathematical texts such as word problems. Some specific language goals include the following:

- Language functions: for example, formulating questions and making predictions based on a math problem
- Language skills: for example, scanning a reading passage and drafting a report or skimming a word problem and sketching a diagram based on the text
- Grammar and language structures: for example, recognizing root words in technical vocabulary
- Understanding tasks needed to complete an assignment: for example, sharing with a partner and counting off by twos

Focusing on rigorous literacy instruction at the same time that we teach mathematics content can help students who lack prior knowledge because of either an interruption in their education or difficulty with the English language. RTI can create a framework for this that structures instruction and assessment around Common Core–based curriculum. This can provide early intervention and prevent academic failure. Let's see what that looks like in Tier 1.

Tier 1 Instruction for English Language Learners

All students, including those whose first language is not English, need instruction consistent with scientifically based, schoolwide interventions that promote understanding of mathematical concepts and is aligned with the Common Core State Standards for mathematics. And regardless of their native language, no two students learn the same way. Curriculum and instruction should incorporate alternatives so that all students, including individuals from various language backgrounds, learning styles, and abilities, have access to materials that match their learning needs and maximize their ability to achieve (Rose & Meyer, 2002). A key principle in RTI is the focus on incorporating prevention and early intervention rather than waiting for failure. Tier 1 is characterized by evidence-based instruction for all students, monitored frequently—at least monthly, but ideally weekly or twice weekly (Fuchs & Fuchs, 2006).

Tier 1 instruction can take place in whole-class or multiple-group formats. A "mathematics classroom should promote dialogues, not monologues" (Brown, Cady, & Taylor, 2009, p. 539). To foster discussion, the classroom should be organized into whole-class, small-group, pair, and other groupings that would allow students to develop interactions with each other. Flexible

Figure 6.1   Sheltered Instruction Observational Protocol Checklist

Lesson Objectives

- ❏ Math
- ❏ Language

Building Background

- ❏ Prior in-school learning
- ❏ Out-of-school knowledge of mathematics

Instructional Scaffolding

- ❏ Modeling mathematical procedures
- ❏ Modeling academic language
- ❏ Guided practice of new math learning
- ❏ Independent practice

Grouping Scaffolding

- ❏ Whole class
- ❏ Small group
- ❏ Pair work
- ❏ Independent work

Language and Mathematics Content Integration

- ❏ Listening
- ❏ Speaking
- ❏ Reading
- ❏ Writing

Practice and Application

- ❏ Hands-on practice
- ❏ Personally and culturally relevant application
- ❏ High level of engagement

Assessment

- ❏ Formative: individual, group
- ❏ Summative
- ❏ Written
- ❏ Oral
- ❏ Electronic

Source: Adapted from Echevarria, Vogt, & Short (2012).

grouping fosters vocabulary acquisition and may facilitate the comfort level of all students in the class. Effective instruction addresses the language, as well as the concepts, of mathematics in the same lesson (see Chapter 5). While this applies to all students, it is even more important for those who are still learning the English language. Focused discourse (i.e., peer-to-peer conversations that are structured to identify and solve problems) should be part of the learning experience for all students, but again, even more so for ELLs (see Chapter 3).

The Sheltered Instruction Observational Protocol (SIOP; Echevarria, Vogt, & Short, 2012) is a research-based instructional framework recommended for Tier 1 content-based and ESL instruction alike. It emphasizes clear content and language objectives, building background knowledge and promoting interaction, research-based instructional strategies, practice, application, and assessment. For purposes of lesson planning and instructional delivery, we recommend this framework since it allows for mathematics instruction to be aligned with these key features.

The checklist in Figure 6.1 (adapted from the SIOP model) can be used as a quick self-assessment tool, or a lesson planning tool, for a teacher's mathematics lesson plan.

While the lesson planning or self-assessment tool presented in Figure 6.1 is designed to be used daily by teachers, we also recommend the implementation of a specific action planner for each tier, which should be used by school-based intervention teams. The action planners in this chapter are based on *A Cultural, Linguistic, and Ecological Framework for Response to Intervention With English Language Learners* (Esparza Brown & Doolittle, 2008).

An effective tool to use at Tier 1 is the action planner presented in Table 6.1.

Table 6.1   Tier 1 Action Planner

Question	Who Is Responsible?	Summary of Notes (Date Completed if Applicable)
Is scientifically based instruction in place for the target student and consideration given to his or her cultural, linguistic, socioeconomic, and experiential background?		

(Continued)

Table 6.1   (Continued)

Question	Who Is Responsible?	Summary of Notes (Date Completed if Applicable)
Is instruction targeted to the student's level of English proficiency?		
Is the concern examined within the context (i.e., language of instruction, acculturation)?		
Have the parents been contacted and their input documented?		
Has accurate baseline data been collected on what the student can do as well as what he or she must still learn?		
Are first and second language proficiency monitored regularly?		
What were the child's preschool literacy experiences, if any?		
Have hearing and vision been screened?		
What tasks can the student perform and in what settings?		
Have specific Tier I RTI interventions that are culturally, linguistically, and experientially appropriate been developed?		

Source: Esparza Brown & Doolittle (2008).

To better visualize what a three-tier intervention in mathematics, specially designed for ELLs and guided by the Common Core, would look like, we invite you to visit a fourth-grade classroom described in the three vignettes presented next.

Common Core Standard for Grade 4 states:

4.MD.2. Use the four operations to solve word problems involving distances, intervals of time, liquid volumes, masses of objects, and money, including problems involving simple fractions or decimals, and problems that require expressing measurements given in a larger unit in terms of a smaller unit. Represent measurement quantities using diagrams such as number line diagrams that feature a measurement scale. (Council of Chief State School Officers, 2010)

Tier 1 Lesson Example

In a fourth-grade class, the teacher introduces the concept of elapsed time by setting the following objectives. Students will be able to

1. find elapsed time, start time, and end time using a time line, clocks, and calculations (content objective) and

2. use past tense verbs correctly to describe past events as well as explain in writing why elapsed time is important in their lives (language objective).

As a warm-up, students work independently to respond in writing to the prompt: *When did you get up today? When did you arrive at school?* To support all levels of language proficiency, students are given sentence starters which they will complete in their notebooks. Next, students form small groups and discuss who has the biggest difference between the two times, or "Who has the longest elapsed time?" Afterward, students report back on how they figured the time difference between getting up and arriving at school, and the teacher defines elapsed time and explicitly models two strategies: using a timeline and subtraction (with and without renaming the time).

In order to transfer the newly gained skills to an authentic context (namely, traveling), students watch a short video clip about the Wright brothers (see www.youtube .com/watch?v=1mQjXUiINh4&feature=related) and predict how long the first flight lasted. Next, the class examines modern-day fight schedules between cities of their choice by searching for flights on the major airlines' websites and recording the take-off and landing times. The elapsed time for each flight is calculated, first as a whole class, then in small groups, while using the key vocabulary: *start time, end time, elapsed time*. For additional practice, students work independently (or in pairs) on

(Continued)

(Continued)

their whiteboards and hold up their responses to questions projected on the SMART Board (if available). To connect math skills to literacy and real-life application, students share the placemat template (see Figure 6.2) and explain why elapsed time is important in their lives by writing or drawing in their own designated section of a placement template. After each section is filled with appropriate responses (drawings, single-word answers, short phrases, sentences, paragraphs), students share and compare what each group member has written and identify the common items in the center of the paper. Students should sit around the rectangular placement to be able to write in their own sections. The placemat can be of any size, but using a large piece of chart paper allows students to easily write their responses in the designated areas (Dove & Honigsfeld, 2013).

Figure 6.2   The Placemat Template

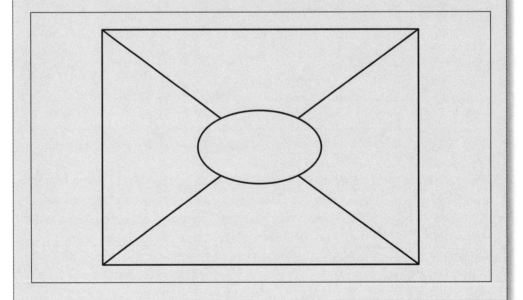

Tier 1 lessons should exemplify best practices in both mathematics education and second language support. They need to be research based, carefully structured, and highly engaging. Here are some guiding principles for Tier 1 interventions:

- Identify a clear goal for each curriculum area: mathematics language and concepts.

- Identify any key vocabulary that may have multiple meanings (social vs. academic) and provide explicit instruction.
- Model appropriate mathematics vocabulary during discussions with the class and the individual student.
- Identify prior experiences as they relate to the students' culture and pose problems in familiar contexts.
- Provide visuals for both instruction and student responses (use manipulative materials whenever possible).
- Avoid using symbols and abbreviations unless the student has a vocabulary chart with the abbreviation or symbol connected to the word it represents.
- New vocabulary should have a minimum of 6 varied exposures during a lesson and ideally a total of 30 or more exposures during the following month. (Capps & Pickreign, 1993)

The recommended time period for measuring response to Tier 1 instruction is 8–10 weeks (Fuchs & Fuchs, 2005). If, after appropriate progress monitoring, the student still does not make adequate progress, he or she should move to Tier 2.

Tier 2 Instruction for English Language Learners

In Tier 2 the intervention should take place in addition to the regular classroom instruction and with a smaller teacher-to-student ratio (four or five students in a group) using different materials and strategies. A challenging question that teachers face in working with ELLs is: Is the child's underlying problem due to lack of (or limited) conceptual understanding of the *math* content, or is there a *language* barrier? We recommend that teachers use specially targeted formative assessments to address both of these potential areas of difficulty. They can help teachers determine (a) the student's current readiness level to work with the target grade-appropriate concepts; (b) how well the child understands the discipline-specific language used in the mathematics lessons; and (c) how comfortable the child is with the general academic language used in word problems, directions given to solve problems, and the typical academic conversations that take place in the class. Based on the answers to these questions, the Tier 2 intervention may target either mathematical concepts and skills or mathematical language acquisition—or both. It is safe to expect that—unless the ELLs had high levels of mathematics instruction in the native language and they are merely working on transferring the skills from one language to another (see Cummins, 2000)—for many students, the challenge might be twofold and more complex than initially anticipated. The most important approach for Tier 2 is providing *explicit instruction,* which is summarized by the National Mathematics Advisory Panel (2008) in the following way:

- Teachers provide clear models for solving a problem type using an array of examples.
- Students receive extensive practice in use of newly learned strategies and skills.
- Students are provided with opportunities to think aloud (i.e., talk through the decisions they make and the steps they take).
- Students are provided with extensive feedback. (p. 23)

See the textbox for a Tier 2 version of the lesson on elapsed time, where the teacher incorporates the National Mathematics Advisory Panel's (2008) recommendations.

Tier 2 Lesson: Elapsed Time Vignette

Tier 2 intervention is based on the work of Barrera et al. (2006) on think-alouds in mathematics instruction. The teacher begins by giving several authentic examples of start times and end times of events that are relevant to the students' lives, such as day at school (When do we get to school and when do we go home?), going to lunch (When do we start lunch and when do we end lunch at school every day?), and so on. While the teacher provides these real-life, concrete examples, he or she uses a variety of manipulatives such as a digital clock to note the start time and the end time of each event and a timeline to show that each event has a beginning and an end and a time span in between those two points, carefully using all the key academic vocabulary relevant to the problems. Thinking aloud about elapsed time, the teacher walks the ELLs through multiple models using the same sentence structure and academic vocabulary for consistency and easier processing. All these initial examples will have whole or half hours and will be calculated without renaming the number. The students are invited to chime in as they start the think-aloud process or to approximate what the teacher is saying while he or she continues to model additional examples (Case, Harris, & Graham, 1992). After extensive modeling and shared think-alouds, the students are put in small groups to work out a problem very similar to the one modeled. They are encouraged to talk and discuss the steps they need to take to figure the answer, while the teacher is available to give extensive feedback or, if needed, "feed forward"—immediate personalized assistance—to each student or group in anticipation of what they might have difficulty with.

Tier 2 interventions will frequently focus on strategies for academic language acquisition. One significant challenge for students learning English is confusion with words used in mathematics that sound like words used in common speech (e.g., *pie* and *pi*) or that have multiple meanings; for example, when students hear the word *sum* or *whole*, they may confuse the words for *some* or *hole* (Pierce & Fontaine, 2009). One strategy a teacher can use is to initiate a discussion on what the class knows the word means in general usage, and then explain how the meaning differs when applied in a mathematics setting. Table 6.2 describes other effective strategies to teach mathematics vocabulary identified by Slavit and Ernst-Slavit (2007).

Similar to Tier 1 interventions, we suggest the use of an action planner for Tier 2 as well, such as the one presented in Table 6.3.

Table 6.2   Effective Strategies to Teach Mathematics Vocabulary

1. Limit the introduction of new vocabulary to fewer than 12 words per lesson (Fathman, Quinn, & Kessler, 1992).
2. Limit the use of idioms.
3. Speak slowly and clearly but with a natural intonation.
4. Use visuals, gestures, realia (real objects), and manipulatives.
5. Break the lesson into smaller units.
6. Pause and stress key terms.
7. Identify words with multiple meanings.
8. Use cognates—a word in one language that is similar in meaning and form to a word in another language; for example, *círculo* means "circle" in Spanish.

Source: Slavit & Ernst-Slavit (2007).

Tier 3 Instruction for English Language Learners

Students that do not make adequate progress in Tier 2 should be moved to Tier 3. This includes one-to-one instruction for increased periods of time in addition to regular work in class, with different materials and different research-based strategies, and may be done by personnel with advanced training. A critical consideration is that lack of fluency in both English and mathematics will require a considerably longer processing time for ELLs. Many students will try to solve a problem in their native language and then attempt to translate the process to English, which means teachers must allow for additional wait time.

Table 6.3 Tier 2 Action Planner

Question	Who Is Responsible?	Summary of Notes (Date Completed if Applicable)
Will instruction in a small-group setting lead to success?		
Has the student's progress been compared to himself or herself using data collected over time and across settings?		
Does the child's learning rate appear to be lower than that of an average-learning "true peer"?		
Is the child responding to interventions?		
Will an alternate curriculum help the student succeed?		
Is scientifically based instruction in place for the target student and consideration given to his or her cultural, linguistic, socioeconomic, and experiential background?		

Source: Esparza Brown & Doolittle (2008).

Many students in Grade 4, both ELLs and English-speaking students for whom English is not the first language, do poorly on the concept of elapsed time and many teachers continue to struggle with finding the most effective way to teach the concept to these students. For Tier 3 intervention, teachers should first reassess the students' prior knowledge for their understanding of temporal relationships (before, after, later, etc.) in English and, if possible, in their native language and encourage students to think about time during the day (Kamii & Russell, 2012). Be sure to review different ways of saying the same time (e.g., 7:45 or "a quarter to eight"), and make sure that students know the terms *morning, noon, afternoon, night, midnight, a.m.,* and *p.m.* Then reassess prior knowledge of seconds, minutes, and hours by asking the following types of questions:

1. How many seconds are in a minute?

2. How many minutes are in an hour?

3. How many minutes are in a half hour?

4. How many hours and minutes are in 92 minutes?

When talking about the difference between the starting time and ending time of an event, it is important to assess the students' understanding of the equivalence of the expressions *time passed* between two times and *elapsed time*. The teacher might use the expression *time passed* when introducing the topic. For example, he or she may say, "If I get up at 7:00 in the morning and do not eat breakfast until 9:00, how much *time passed* before I ate breakfast?" The mathematical term *elapsed time* should then be introduced and the same sentence discussed with the students substituting the expression *elapsed time* for *time passed*.

Students should be encouraged to think about the duration of time throughout the day. Asking a question like "What time did you eat breakfast this morning?" or "What time did you leave for school this morning?" is helpful to encourage student thinking about the concept of time. This can also be accomplished by having students move the hands on a large demonstration clock to show how much time has passed while encouraging conversation about the duration of time. In addition, we can ask questions such as these:

1. Do we have enough time to read a story before lunch begins at 11:17? (It is 10:45 now . . .)

2. If each person gets 10 minutes to give a book report, how much time will be needed for 7 reports? (Kamii & Russell, 2012, p. 312)

At various times throughout the day, ask the student to tell what time is shown on the classroom clock.

Consistent with the Common Core State Standards, some students may respond to a lesson using an adapted number line to evaluate elapsed time. Our Tier 3 lesson uses a number line to provide a more concrete representation of the abstract concept of time and is based on the work of Kamii and Russell (2012). In this lesson the teacher can demonstrate how to use the adapted number line to calculate how much time there is between two points in a time line. This lesson demonstrates time in a visual manner using a number line. Draw a number line on the board from 1 through 12, equally spaced. (There are also apps for the whiteboard that will create a number line to use for time.) Next, create a chart on the blackboard or whiteboard as in Table 6.4.

Have the student fill in the chart with activities of their choice that take 1 hour to accomplish. For each activity, draw a line between two numbers on your number line "clock." Continue this process using different

Table 6.4   Table of Time-Based Activities

Activity	Start Time	End Time	Elapsed Time
Homework	6:00	7:00	1 hour

Figure 6.3   Adapted Number Line to Teach Elapsed Time

activities and numbers on the number line. This will help students view time as a familiar "time/number" line in a linear format. Figure 6.3 shows the number line clock for the activity of doing homework from 6 o'clock to 7 o'clock.

Repeat the process by adding vertical lines between numbers representing half hour, then 15 minutes, and so on.

Next, give the student 12 index cards, 12 paper fasteners, and a magic marker. Number the cards from 1 to 12 on the left-hand portion of one side. Fasten the cards together in order to form a circle, and connect the first and the last card to change the number line into a circle that makes up the face of a clock. The number line now becomes a clock. This will visually assist students in making the transition between the linear time/number line they have become familiar with and the circular time/number line of a clock. Go through the chart activities and have the students trace the elapsed time on the cards with their finger, then fill in the last column with the elapsed time. As the students become more proficient, the chart in Figure 6.3 can be duplicated with activities that take more than an hour. Half hours (30 minutes) and quarter hours (15 minutes) can be added to the cards.

Finally, the action planner for Tier 3 interventions will specifically address previous interventions as well as students' responses to them (see Table 6.5).

It is important for all students, but especially ELLs, to have opportunities to listen, speak, read, and write in mathematics classes, with teachers providing appropriate support and encouragement (NCTE, 2008).

Table 6.5   Tier 3 Action Planner

Question	Who Is Responsible?	Summary of Notes (Date Completed if Applicable)
How many rounds of Tier 2 instruction has the student had?		
Is there evidence of progress from previous interventions?		
Is the student successful with different curriculum, teaching approaches, and an individualized setting?		
Does the student differ from like "true peers" in the following ways: • Level of performance? • Learning slope?		
What are the child's functional, developmental, academic, linguistic, and cultural needs?		
If additional assessments are used, are the instruments technically sound, valid, and used appropriately for the ELL?		
Are test results interpreted in a manner that considers the student's language proficiency in first and second language and their level of acculturation?		
Do assessments include information in the student's home language and English?		
Has the student received continuous instruction (i.e., absences do not make up a good portion of the student's profile)?		

Source: Esparza Brown & Doolittle (2008).

Tech Byte

MATHEMATICS FOR
ENGLISH LANGUAGE LEARNERS

www.tsusmell.org/index.htm

The Mathematics for English Language Learners (MELL) project is a comprehensive research initiative focused on creating instructional tools for K–12 educators teaching mathematics to ELLs. The MELL project is facilitated by the Texas State University System in partnership with the Texas Education Agency and K–12 educators. The site (see Figure 6.4) contains resources, information about online and face-to-face professional development, videos of different types of manipulatives to introduce or reinforce key mathematical concepts, and conference information. The site also contains a lesson plan bank and print resources for teaching mathematics to ELLs (see Figure 6.5). The series of online learning videos provides strategies for teachers and preservice teachers to reach all students, not only those for whom their first language is not English.

Each category on the blue bar has a pull down menu with additional categories of resources. By clicking on Resources, the Products and Resource Page appears (see Figure 6.5).

Also under Resources is Useful Links, which contains many resources especially for students for whom Spanish is a first language (see Figure 6.6).

Figure 6.4   MELL Website Home Page

Source: http://www.tsusmell.org

Figure 6.5   MELL Products and Resources Page

Source: http://www.tsusmell.org/resources/mell-resources.htm

Figure 6.6   MELL Website Resources Page

Source: http://www.tsusmell.org/resources/useful-links.htm

The resources available on this website are too numerous to mention. Teachers will find it helpful for both additional lesson plans for the classroom and professional development for themselves.

Resources for Further Study

Mathematics, the Common Core, and Language

http://ell.stanford.edu/publication/mathematics-common-core-and-language

Judit Moschkovich makes recommendations for developing mathematics instruction for ELLs aligned with the Common Core State Standards in a short video and in a downloadable paper. The recommendations can help teachers support mathematical reasoning for their students.

Moschkovich, J. N. (2009). *Using Two Languages When Learning Mathematics: How Can Research Help Us Understand Mathematics Learners Who Use Two Languages?*

www.nctm.org/uploadedFiles/Research_News_and_Advocacy/Research/Clips_and_Briefs/Research_brief_12_Using_2.pdf

This research brief summarizes how students who are bilingual or learning English use two languages and how this knowledge can assist the classroom teacher in helping these students master mathematics concepts.

TeacherTube

www.teachertube.com/viewVideo.php?title=Elapsed_Time&video_id=160958

This is a link to a short video that describes one strategy to teach elapsed time, using a T chart.

Glossary

ELL (English Language Learner): An active learner of the English language who may benefit from various types of language support programs. This term is used mainly in the United States to describe K–12 students.

ESL (English as a Second Language): Formerly used to designate ELLs, this term increasingly refers to a program of instruction designed to support ELLs. It is still used to refer to multilingual students in higher education.

LEP (Limited English Proficiency): Employed by the U.S. Department of Education to refer to ELLs who lack sufficient mastery of English to meet state standards and excel in an English-language classroom. Increasingly, *English language learner* is used to describe this population, because it highlights learning, rather than suggesting that nonnative-English-speaking students are deficient.

7

Teaching Mathematics in an Inclusion Classroom Guided by the Common Core

Every child has a different learning style and pace. Each child is unique, not only capable of learning but also capable of succeeding.

—Robert John Meehan

In this chapter you will learn:

- The relationships among the Common Core State Standards, Response to Intervention (RTI), and inclusion as a single educational program within a school
- How to prepare to teach mathematics content guided by the Common Core State Standards within an RTI framework, in an inclusion setting
- Specific techniques that can be used to teach mathematics guided by the Common Core State Standards in a Tier 1 inclusion setting that benefit both general education and special education students
- Specific techniques that can be used to teach mathematics guided by the Common Core State Standards in a Tier 2 small-group inclusion setting and Tier 3 individual instruction

Susan James is beginning her fourth year teaching middle school math. She has just received tenure and is beginning to see herself as an experienced, if not yet a master teacher. Now, just as she is gaining some confidence, her department chair tells her she is assigned to team teach a sixth-grade inclusion class with a special education teacher. Susan is nervous, but fortunately her new partner, Melanie Scott, has had 2 years' experience with the team teaching inclusion format, and after their first planning session, Susan is feeling more comfortable with the learning curve that lies before her.

Melanie has been teaching special education for 12 years and was a member of the task force that introduced RTI to her school 2 years ago. Since then, she has team taught the history and social studies curriculum which included the Common Core State Standards for literacy. She developed an approach that combines the three state-mandated reforms (RTI, CCSS, and inclusion) into a single coherent process. Now the new team will combine Susan's knowledge of mathematics instruction and Melanie's expertise in special education to teach mathematics in an inclusion class guided by the Common Core.

For over a century, American schools organized their educational system by creating separate groups of students, based on levels of academic performance. The move toward inclusion is reversing this, bringing a wide range of students together into a single class and requiring teachers to develop the interpersonal skills to work effectively with diverse students, at the same time that they are teaching a far broader range of academic interventions.

The Hierarchy of Relationships Among RTI, the Common Core, and Inclusion

As described in Chapter 2, RTI and the Common Core State Standards need to be seen not as individual programs, but as interdependent parts of a single educational paradigm. In this chapter we will expand that paradigm to include another mandated component of American education: inclusion.

Since the 1990 reauthorization of the Individuals with Disabilities Education Act (IDEA), inclusion of virtually every student into general education classes, alongside general education students, has evolved into a civil right guaranteed by federal and state law. The arguments behind a child's right to inclusion are the same as those used more than 50 years ago in *Brown v. Board of Education* that required integration of all races into American schools (Karagiannis, Stainback, & Stainback, 1996). This monumental ruling was based as much on educational psychology as on constitutional requirements for equal protection. In reaching its decision, the Supreme Court found that the "separate but equal" argument did not apply in the area of education because forced separation of groups of students from the perceived mainstream produced irreparable psychological and emotional damage. The studies of Kenneth Clark (Clark & Clark, 1950) and others persuaded the court that forced segregation of children made equal opportunity and equal education impossible to achieve in a segregated setting, regardless of any other factors that may be present (Beggs, 1995).

Supporters of inclusion for special needs students used the same argument during the 1980s and 1990s (Connor & Ferri, 2007). Debates that led to reauthorizations of IDEA in 1990, 1997, and 2004 claimed that when children with special needs received their education in settings removed from the general student population, they suffered irreparable psychological damage that was generally not outweighed by the advantages of instruction in smaller self-contained classes. During the 1990s, IDEA redefined the term *least restrictive environment* (LRE) to mean specifically "alongside students without disabilities" (Karagiannis et al., 1996, p. 17); in other words, for all but the most exceptionally disabled students, the goal of special education is to provide services specifically in general education classes (U.S. Department of Education, n.d.). This was a sharp departure from the previous use of the term LRE to mean only the least restrictive setting that best serves a child's individual needs, with no specific reference to the general education classroom.

As of 2011, more than half (58%) of special education students spent at least 80% of their school day in general education classes (Snyder & Dillow, 2012). This has enormous implications for teachers and administrators as they prepare to introduce Common Core content into their schools using the Response to Intervention process. It means that inclusion needs to be seen as a central part of the unified RTI–Common Core State Standards implementation process.

We can illustrate how inclusion fits into the RTI–Common Core model (described in Chapter 2, Figure 2.3) with the expanded diagram shown in Figure 7.1.

The illustration in Figure 7.1 is based on Maslow's (1943) bottom-to-top hierarchy of interdependent needs. Starting with the foundation at the bottom, each successive stage depends on fulfilling the ones below. Academic achievement (the *outcome*) depends on students learning the curriculum based on the Common Core State Standards (the *content*), which, in turn, depends on the effective use of RTI (the *process*) for the instruction for all students (see Chapter 2, Figure 2.3). Here, as a prerequisite to RTI and the Common Core, we have the additional elements of inclusion classes and individualized instruction (the *setting*), which complete the hierarchy.

Figure 7.1   RTI, Common Core, and Inclusion as an Integrated Process

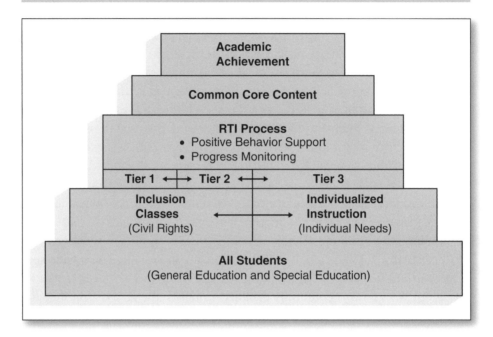

A Note of Caution in the Inclusion Process

It is important to note three aspects of the inclusion-individualized instruction interrelationship shown in Figure 7.1.

First, the standard of ensuring inclusion in general education classes should not be seen as necessarily the best outcome for every student, without exception. Neither inclusion nor individualization (one-to-one instruction, resource room, or self-contained classes) should be seen as an absolute goal. While inclusion is a civil right of every student, and the great majority of students benefit from it, many students do need the special advantages (such as teachers with specific specialized training) that can come only outside of the mainstream setting, at least for a time (Schneider, 2009). One of the serious mistakes of well-intentioned educators is overgeneralization of benefits: They implement an inclusion program based on a philosophy that inclusion should be the goal for all students at all times. While every student is *entitled* to inclusion, not every student will actually *benefit* from it. In fact, there will always be some students whose individual needs, at certain times, will require instruction in a special setting outside the mainstream (Bateman & Bateman, 2001). One of the advantages of the RTI process, with its reliance on formative assessment and data, is to alert teachers and administrators to when the general education process is not working and then guide the teachers' choice of effective alternative interventions—based on individual student needs—before there is a history of failure. The ideals of inclusion should not blind us to our obligation to provide for these needs, even when it means the temporary use of specialized individualized instruction, resource room services, or a self-contained class apart from the mainstream. It is often necessary to more intensively assess and build the prerequisite skills needed to obtain a specific Common Core State Standard goal that will allow the student to ultimately benefit from inclusion in the general education classroom.

Another caution relates to an idea expressed by some researchers and echoed by parents and teachers. Even for the majority of children who could benefit from inclusion, when teachers are not properly prepared, the program can do more harm than good (Khan, 2012; Zubal-Ruggieri & Smith, 2003). As NASA engineers and supervisors learned during the 1986 flight of Challenger, if preparations for a launch are not complete, or if deadlines become more important than the integrity of the program, the outcome can be disaster. Administrators and teachers need to be keenly aware of their own knowledge base and the readiness of their school before implementing an inclusion program. Neither the Common Core State Standards nor RTI can work in an inclusion setting if the program is not well designed or the professional staff is not fully trained and prepared.

This leads to an additional aspect of the interrelationship between RTI, the Common Core State Standards, and inclusion: Many children will need to move freely within the range of settings and services of inclusion, just as they do among the tiers of RTI. The horizontal arrows in Figure 7.1 illustrate this. As we have seen in Chapter 2, RTI is an inherently flexible process, not a fixed program, and students can and should move within the three tiers. As we discussed in our work on Universal Design for Learning, the emphasis is on adjusting the educational process to meet the needs of each child, rather than fitting all students into a preexisting program or educational philosophy. Here, the use of language can make a noticeable difference in the way teachers, administrators, students, and parents perceive what is happening in an RTI–Common Core–inclusion continuum. The expression "a Tier 3 student" fixes the special services of Tier 3 as part of the child's identity, while "a student in Tier 3" implies that the child will eventually move to Tier 2 or 1. One of the benefits of viewing RTI, the Common Core State Standards, and inclusion as parts of a single unified process is the openness to growth based on individual development, rather than a series of fixed placements within distinct programs.

TEACHING THE COMMON CORE STATE STANDARDS FOR MATHEMATICS CONTENT WITHIN AN RTI FRAMEWORK IN AN INCLUSION SETTING

Susan, the mathematics teacher, and Melanie, the special education teacher, meet several weeks before their classroom partnership is scheduled to begin. After coffee and comparing experiences with their own preschool children at home, Melanie tells Susan about the 2 years she has spent working with a social studies teacher in an inclusion class. She suggests that strategies she learned from these experiences might be helpful and she would be happy to share them with Susan as she and Susan develop their own inclusion class strategies. Sharing might create an easier transition from solo teaching to co-teaching than it would have been if both were starting from the beginning.

Susan agrees and through several conversations learns that the three most important elements in the co-teaching process are joint preparation time, having a wide and deep library of alternative interventions readily available when they are needed, and the ability to adapt quickly when experience shows that a plan is not working well. (Susan comments that these are generally the opposite of the approaches she learned years ago in teacher education, where she was taught to prepare her own lesson plans, base them on the curriculum provided by her school's mathematics department, and follow them as designed without variation.) As in any effective teaching, both teachers need to have a clear understanding of the Common Core State Standard(s) that will guide the lesson and especially of the conceptual basis of the mathematical concept addressed.

Melanie then asks if Susan can schedule time together before each lesson to review the mathematics curriculum content that will be covered. She explains that this will be the starting point when she, as the special education teacher, will need to modify the assignments and homework for individual students who will need these adjustments. She may also suggest some flexible instructional approaches to engage all the students, including those in the general population. Susan mentions that, unlike the social studies curriculum that Melanie is familiar with, mathematics is precise and cumulative: The curriculum is guided by deep conceptual understandings identified in the Common Core State Standards, and instruction in mathematics topics depends on prerequisite skills developed in earlier lessons and perhaps previous grades. She explains that this will require the two teachers to modify work even more carefully than they would in a social studies, English, or even science curriculum, where there may be more flexibility in adjusting the specific academic content and format while still meeting Common Core State Standards.

The earlier and following chapters expand on the Common Core State Standards and RTI (the *what* and the *how*); this chapter focuses on the particular needs of mathematics instruction in an inclusion setting (the *where*).

It is not surprising that inclusion is among the most difficult and challenging developments in modern education. By definition, it calls for teachers to move beyond their comfort zone and, in many cases, beyond their training and certification areas. In almost every state, teachers need to have a specialized certification in order to serve as the teacher of record for students formally classified for special education and receiving services governed by an individual education plan (IEP). At the same time, most states also have a complex of regulations governing the academic coursework in the subject area, which teachers are required to complete to be certified to teach particular academic subjects to any students, general or special education, at various grade levels.

> To review, our unified hierarchy of mathematics instruction in an inclusive setting:
>
> - **The Common Core State Standards** are the benchmarks for the content of instruction. They tell us *what* we teach.
> - **Response to Intervention** is the framework for instruction. It tells us *how* we teach and assess.
> - **Inclusion** is the setting and context for instruction. It tells us *where* we teach.

These regulations make it unlikely that most special education teachers would have the coursework concentration and the experiences during their preservice or in-service training needed to teach mathematics to an inclusive class of general education and special education students on their own. For this reason, the most common format for inclusive instruction has involved some form of co-teaching (Kloo & Zigmond, 2008). The idea is known under a growing number of terms, including *team teaching, shared instructional responsibility, collaborative teaching, instructional consultation,* and others (Muller, Friend, & Hurley-Chamberlain, 2009). No matter what term is used, the process calls for general education specialists in academic areas (such as mathematics) to team up with certified special education teachers to teach a blended group of students for which neither professional would possess the certification or perhaps the skills to teach on his or her own (Friend & Hurley-Chamberlain, 2008; Hang & Rabren, 2009; Scruggs, Mastropieri, & McDuffie, 2007).

The exception to this would be teachers who have completed duel certification preservice teacher education programs or additional coursework to become certified in both mathematics and special education. A number of graduate and undergraduate programs offer degrees that lead to duel certification.

In the absence of duel certification, co-teaching offers a number of clear benefits:

- It provides deeper mathematical experiences for special needs students than some special education teachers may be able to offer.
- It gives general education teachers the insights and support they may need to better differentiate instruction for students with special needs.
- It reduces the stigma that many special needs students experience in self-contained classes and expands the experiences of general education students. (Murawski, 2008)

Susan and Melanie have been co-teaching their mathematics inclusion class for 3 months and have become close friends as well as professional colleagues. They have developed insight into each other's capabilities, shortcomings, and personal style. As with most successful co-teaching partnerships, theirs is based on strong mutual respect and friendship that allows each partner to produce a higher level of work than would be possible alone.

In this case, Susan and Melanie have adapted their different styles of teaching that complement one another. Susan, the mathematics teacher, previously believed that intensive practice was the best approach to developing skills in the basic operations that her students need. After some uncomfortable moments, she learned from Melanie that, for students who have difficulty with visual distractions, less is more. One or two problems on a page, printed in an 18-point sans serif font, produce more learning than 10 problems printed in 12-point font. At the same time, Melanie, the special education teacher, has become much more attuned than she had been while teaching social studies to the necessity of addressing the prior skills that are the foundation for the deep understandings in mathematics required by the Common Core State Standards. When she needs to modify a homework assignment, she now uses her creativity to search for new approaches to presenting the required content, rather than merely finding different examples, as she had in the past. She has also learned the value of frequent short formative assessments to guide her instruction. More important, both teachers have learned that co-teaching mathematics opens the door to varieties of teaching opportunities that would never be possible as a solo teacher.

Researchers have reported on forms of co-teaching since the mid-1990s (e.g., Friend & Cook, 1995; Scruggs et al., 2007). Table 7.1 summarizes six of the most common approaches.

Table 7.1 Approaches to Co-Teaching and Appropriate Roles and Tasks

Approaches to Co-Teaching	Appropriate Uses
1. Teach—Observe Teacher 1: Teaches academic content. Teacher 2: Observes and takes notes on student responses.	• Initial diagnosis of student needs. • Progress check. • Comparison of student responses.
2. Teach—Drift and Support Teacher 1: Teaches academic content. Teacher 2: Drifts among class offering unobtrusive support to individual students in need without distinction between those in general and special education.	• Lesson content requires the expertise of Teacher 1. • Teacher 2 is new to the program or inexperienced in the lesson content. • Lesson requires intensive support for certain students.
3. Parallel Teaching Teacher 1 and Teacher 2 share the teaching, presenting the lesson as a team or alternating the presentations in a "tag-team" format.	• Class is experienced and comfortable with the teaching team. • Academic content lends itself to team instruction (this can be a difficult determination). • Lower teacher-to-student ratio leads to more efficient instruction.
4. Station Teaching Teacher 1: Teaches academic content for one part of the lesson. Teacher 2: Teaches academic content for a second part of the lesson. Students rotate between Teacher 1 and Teacher 2, having access to each as needed.	• Academic content is complex and sequential, but not hierarchical. • Instruction calls for application of concepts or frequent review and application. • Content has several distinct topics.
5. Alternative Teaching *Before Class* Teacher 1 and Teacher 2 co-plan the lesson, dividing the content between a larger group receiving a more advanced form of the lesson and a smaller group receiving a more basic version. *During Class* Teacher 1: Teaches the advanced group.	• Academic content is complex and sequential, but not hierarchical. • Instruction calls for application of concepts or frequent review and application. • Content has several distinct topics. • Student skills show great variation. • There is concern that high-performing students may lose educational opportunity in a unified lesson.

(Continued)

Table 7.1   (Continued)

Approaches to Co-Teaching	Appropriate Uses
Teacher 2: Teaches the basic group. The division into groups could be for the entire lesson or only a portion. *After Class* Team meets and analyzes data.	• Struggling students require special or intensive support.
6. Back-and-Forth Conversational Teaching *Before Class* Teacher 1 and Teacher 2 co-plan the lesson, dividing the content between their areas of expertise. *During Class* Teacher 1 and Teacher 2 teach the academic content using brief, alternating conversational exchanges. Exchanges can be spontaneous or well scripted, but must be carefully planned to cover the required content. *After Class* Team meets and analyzes data.	• Teachers' expertise is comparable and experience supports one another. • Teachers are experienced and comfortable working together. Should not be used during the early weeks of a partnership. • Students are familiar and comfortable with the team and will see the interactions as mutual support for the lesson content rather than potential conflict or confusion. • Goal of the lesson includes a demonstration of how interaction can lead to enhanced learning.

Source: Friend & Cook (1995); Scruggs, Mastropieri, & McDuffie (2007).

Co-teaching is a partnership, a professional "marriage." It is a delicate balance of complimentary professional and interpersonal skills between two (or more) individuals as they work together with the same students. The team element expands the capabilities of both individuals, but this advantage comes only when the two teachers' interpersonal relationship is equal to their academic and teaching skills. This takes time and careful preparation, and one of the most common causes of breakdown in new co-teaching programs is a failure in these areas. Preparation includes attention to structure and logistics as well as selecting professionals who share teaching philosophies and commitment to the idea of team teaching. The logistics include things like common preparation time and careful arrangement of schedules. Selection of compatible professionals includes interviews involving both teachers, focused on open discussion of their teaching styles, goals for students, and ability to make adjustments in their approaches to classroom instruction. Unfortunately, not every co-teaching classroom is set up to create the level of partnership necessary to maximize the benefits of this approach. On occasion a co-teaching team may meet for the first time on the first day of school or not be scheduled with common planning periods to collaborate, plan, and structure the responsibilities for each member of the team. If teachers cannot discuss and collaborate outside of class, a large portion of the benefits of the co-teaching model for their students inside class are likely to be lost. Table 7.2 illustrates a typical division of roles and responsibilities found in a co-teaching setting.

Both teachers must be experts in the Common Core State Standards for mathematics, the content appropriate for the grade level they are teaching, and the deep conceptual understanding of mathematics that the Common Core State Standards required for their students to gain the maximum benefit from a co-teaching environment.

Teaching Mathematics in a Tier 1 Inclusion Setting

Tier 1 is the foundation of RTI, the framework for implementing the Common Core, and a starting point for an effective inclusion program. It is based on the maxim "diagnose before you prescribe"—never begin working with a

Table 7.2   Possible Roles of Co-Teachers in a Mathematics Class

The general educator uses his or her expertise in:	*The special educator uses his or her expertise in:*
Learning strategies to address the diverse learning needs in mathematics for general education students	Learning strategies to address the unique learning needs of special needs students in the area of mathematics
The district and state mathematics curriculum	Writing and monitoring IEP goals and objectives for individualizing mathematics instruction
Developing the pacing and sequencing of mathematics instruction to meet general education goals	Case management and progress monitoring
Knowledge of the typical learner, social and behavioral characteristics for a large group of students at a grade level	Understanding the learning process for mathematics that needs to be matched appropriately to each learner's characteristics
The mathematics content areas	Accommodations and modifications needed for individual learners

Source: Adapted from Maryland Learning Links (http://marylandlearninglinks.org).

class or a student before prescreening them to determine their levels of proficiency in the topic and in the prerequisite skills needed for success with a new topic. We do this routinely at the beginning of each school year in the initial screening stage of progress monitoring (see Chapter 4). Universal screening is especially important at the lower grades because of the importance of prior knowledge for the understanding of higher mathematics concepts. Information on screening tools and processes for grades up to Grade 3 can be found in *Screening for Mathematics Difficulties in K–3 Students* (Gersten, Clarke, Haymond, & Jordan, 2011).

The screening process should include prerequisite skills needed for each Common Core State Standard for mathematics for the unit of study or grade level. These are the concepts that students need to understand before they are capable of developing a new specific skill. For example, in the State of Maryland, Grade K, Standard 1.0 (Knowledge of Algebra, Patterns, Functions), Objective b (*Represent and analyze repeating patterns using no more than 3 objects in the core of the pattern*), these are the prerequisite skills required before a student is considered prepared to begin the learning process:

> Before students are able to copy and repeat patterns, experiences with sorting, classifying, and ordering must be done. Sorting activities allow young learners to isolate specific attributes while recognizing likenesses and differences among objects. For example, buttons may be sorted by a common color or shape or by the number of holes. Classifying provides learners with the opportunity to name the common or contrasting attributes of an object, such as *buttons without a circular face or buttons with two colors.*
>
> Additionally, ordering objects is another skill which prepares students to copy and repeat patterns. Tasks that reinforce the skill of ordering may include the arrangement of objects from largest to smallest, sequencing daily events, and counting. Finally, songs and poems with a repetitive quality expose learners to the recursive nature of patterns through auditory experiences. (Maryland State Department of Education, 1997–2013)

Teamwork, Consultation, and Lesson Modification

In an inclusion mathematics class, lesson modification involves not only the standard elements of progress monitoring, but consultation between the general education and special education teachers to review the prerequisite skills of each special and general education student. For many students, learning involves more than purely academic interventions and includes learning styles, processing needs, behavior analysis, positive behavioral support, and sensory sensitivities (heightened sensitivity to environmental stimuli, such as lighting, noise, or visual distractions). If the co-teaching model in the school provides for two teachers in the classroom, students, both general education and those with special needs, may spend time in smaller groups based on similar needs for prerequisite skills or learning style modifications. One teacher can work with each group. Some typical or general education students may not come with all the prerequisite skills necessary for success, so the groups may be a mix of general education students and students with special needs.

Also, teachers need to plan how they will modify instruction, classwork, and homework if needed for each student so that the academic content is presented in a way that every student can comprehend. Lesson modification is especially critical in mathematics because of the need to balance the precision of the academic content with the wide range of learning needs found in special education students. More than in almost any other subject, modification of mathematics lessons calls for equal partnership between the academic teacher, who must ensure that the content is presented with technical accuracy, and the special education teacher, who is responsible for making certain that the academic precision is available in a form the student can grasp. Lesson and homework modification is one of the most critical aspects of inclusion in mathematics; it should be approached with great attention to detail and also sensitivity and responsiveness to the way each student reacts to the modifications.

One of the key elements for success in team teaching is beyond the power of most teachers to control: the need for *common planning time* that will allow teachers to consult regularly—ideally, daily—on the balance between whole-class instruction and individual support that will be needed for each lesson, and on the role that each teacher will play in the day's activities. In most cases, the administrators and supervisors are the individuals responsible to make certain that the opportunity for common planning is built into a school's schedule. Providing this opportunity may not ensure the success of an inclusion program, but *not providing common planning time will all but guarantee its failure*.

Also, inclusion is not a process that can be easily standardized; working with each student involves a degree of trial-and-error adjustment until an effective approach to presenting mathematics is reached. For example, the mathematics and special education teachers in this chapter's scenario are working with a student who has a diagnosis of Asperger syndrome. Susan (the mathematics teacher) developed a homework assignment as a review of several Common Core State Standards for Grades 4 and 5. She asks Melanie (the special education teacher) to modify the homework assignment sheet shown in Figure 7.2 for the student.

Figure 7.2   Homework Assignment

Name: _____

Math—Homework

Directions: Solve the problem.

1)   498   2)   1,589
     × 67   − 542
    _____   _____

What time do you see on the clock?

_____

What time will it be in 1 hour?_____

What time was it 1 hour ago?_____

Round 9,321 to the nearest thousand (circle the answer).
     9,000   or   8,000

Round 342 to the nearest hundred (circle the answer).
     300   or   400

Melanie points out several areas that are likely to be difficult or confusing to a person with Asperger syndrome. These students will typically have difficulty with graphomotor skills, such as aligning numbers in columns for multiplication and subtraction. They also need to follow familiar routines and to think literally; they often have difficulty interpreting language that is in any way figurative or abstract. She suggests making the modifications shown in Figure 7.3.

Figure 7.3   Modified Homework Assignment

Name: _____

Math—Homework

Directions: Solve the problem.

1)   498
    ×   67

2)   1,589
   −   542

What time do you see on the clock?

_____

What time will it be in 1 hour later?_____

What time was it 1 hour before?_____

Round 9,321 to the nearest thousand (circle the answer).

    8,000   or   9,000

Round 342 to the nearest hundred (circle the answer).

    300   or   400

The homework assignment was a quick review of prerequisite skills. For the multiplication and subtraction problems (CCSS Grade 5: *Fluently multiply multi-digit whole numbers using the standard algorithm*; CCSS Grade 4: *Fluently add and subtract multi-digit whole numbers using the standard algorithm*), Melanie has added a grid of lines to help the student organize the numbers of the calculation into clear rows and columns. (She also suggests using large-scale graph paper.) She points out that the expressions "in one hour" and "one hour ago" are easily understood by typical students but that a student with Asperger syndrome is likely to find them confusing since they are difficult to understand literally. She suggests changing them to "one hour later" and "one hour before." Finally, she points out that in the rounding question (CCSS Grade 4: *Use place value understanding to round multi-digit whole numbers to any place*), the choices are in reverse order than they would appear on the number lines that all students are familiar with (number lines are almost always arranged with the lower values to the left and the higher to the right). A student with Asperger syndrome will likely be confused by the reverse arrangement, particularly when the second problem presents the selection in the familiar order.

These simple modifications have no effect on the mathematical content of the lesson but can make a huge difference in the response of students with specific learning needs.

Prior to the start of an inclusion program and the gathering of benchmark academic data, the teachers should review what is known about each special needs student in the areas of learning needs, learning styles, behavior, and sensory sensitivity: Which approaches and environmental surroundings is the student most responsive to? Which should be avoided? This can provide valuable insight into selecting the initial approach to math instruction, the reasons for students' reaction to instruction, and can guide decisions on alternative interventions should these be needed. Universal screening results for the general education students in the class should be analyzed for areas of difficulty and possible needs for reteaching of prerequisite skills.

Preparing a General Education Mathematics Class for Inclusion

After the general education mathematics teacher and special education teacher consult and are prepared to work as a team, the next step in the inclusion process is to prepare the students. Both general education and special needs students need to know what changes from their previous school experiences they can expect. There may be changes in classroom routines, differences in learning materials based on individual learning styles or needs, and differences in teacher-to-student ratio if there is a co-teacher or teaching assistant assigned to the inclusion class. As with work modification, this is not a process that can be standardized and applied to each setting according to set rules. The goal is to prepare students for adjustments to their routine and differences they may observe in classmates in an inclusive class. For some students in some schools, this will involve very little change and little preparation will be needed; for others, the alterations may be significant and a great deal of attention will have to be given to the preparation. In either case, the teachers will need to base their approach to the students not on ideals of inclusive behavior, but on the realities of the experiences and expectation of each student in the class. This discussion could include activities that encourage students to feel comfortable with diversity and see the inherent value of all individuals, including those who look different from themselves or have challenges. Children's books may help to start these discussions.

Preparation for inclusion begins with an understanding of the foundations of learning. Lilian Katz (1989) described four elements of the learning process that can help in teaching students to accept, and eventually enjoy, being with one another. Teachers can readily apply these to the type of learning needed to develop an inclusive class in mathematics:

1. *Knowledge*: Acquiring information, facts, and concepts about other students—their background, abilities, disabilities, behaviors. General education students are taught that a student with Asperger syndrome can be exceptionally good at mathematics calculations but have difficulty explaining how he or she solved a problem and tends to become frustrated when other students can't find an answer as quickly as he or she does. The student with Asperger syndrome may learn that many of the general education students are slower to solve problems but can be better than he or she is at explaining how to do them.

2. *Skills*: Actions or behaviors, such as explaining the solution to a math problem, that are observable, measurable, and performed in specific periods of time. A general education student may possess the knowledge that a classmate with Down syndrome needs to have the steps to an addition problem explained in a certain sequence. However, they may not be aware that the classmate also needs to develop the skills that will allow him or her to follow a sequence that is different than the one already known.

3. *Dispositions*: Habits of thinking and tendencies to act in certain ways, such as the disposition to enjoy solving mathematics problems or an aversion to mathematics. A student may have developed the knowledge and skills needed to divide fractions, but exhibits a negative disposition to the task and does not complete homework. Dispositions can provide explanations for student behaviors, both toward their work and toward their classmates.

4. *Feelings*: Subjective emotions that can be either inborn or acquired through the development of knowledge, skills, and dispositions. Feelings of security, loneliness, confidence, fear, compassion, revulsion, and empathy are found in any typical class of students. These drive human behavior far more readily than the higher order rational processes, but can be influenced by careful attention to knowledge, skills, and dispositions (Kahneman, 2011). General education students may feel uncomfortable in the company

of a student with autism, and the student with autism may feel fearful of classmates who interact with one another in ways that he or she is not able. These feelings are powerful, driving student behavior, but they can be influenced by teachers who carefully prepare discussions and activities that increase students' knowledge of one another, their skills in interacting, and their habits of mind or dispositions toward one another.

Griffith, Cooper, and Ringlaben (2002) have adapted these four components of learning to a three-phase approach—what they call the 3-D Model—which can be helpful to teachers in preparing students for an inclusion class.

Phase 1-D focuses on the dispositions and feelings of students toward their new classmates, particularly friendliness and caring. In the same way that students who like baseball are more likely to feel comfortable with a mathematical problem about batting averages, students are more comfortable talking to classmates whom they have some positive feeling for. Feelings and dispositions usually drive knowledge, rather than the reverse (Kahneman, 2011). The first phase of developing an inclusion class is to promote activities and discussions that focus on qualities of students that their peers will find appealing. This can be an opportunity for implementing the Common Core State Standards principles for mathematical practice focused on problem solving. For example, the teacher may design word problems that relate to members of the class and focus on ethnic, cultural, or challenge-based differences among them. A group activity might ask students to survey the class and report on various statistical parameters, such as family size, ethnic backgrounds, and so on. Students can also create their own story problems based on experiences in their native country, then share them with their classmates to solve as a group.

Often we shy away from things that are not familiar to us. Maintaining an open and nonthreatening environment in the classroom may encourage sharing of differences and may lead to an awareness of similarities among students. Note that these, and any activities designed to sensitize students to differences among them, need to be planned with great care and sensitivity to individual student situations. Teachers should be aware of any areas of individual students' lives that they would not want discussed with the group, such as an absentee parent or recent death in the family. As with every aspect of individualized planning, "off the shelf" programs and planning need to be replaced by an understanding of each student's unique needs and circumstances.

Phase 2-D focuses on students' knowledge and understanding of one another. Teachers design activities that teach students about differences between themselves and their classmates. This knowledge is an essential part of positive relationships among students, but it is not enough. Students need to know what specific behaviors these differences are likely to produce in their classmates and why it is happening. A student with Tourette syndrome may predictably exhibit unusual, even bizarre, outbursts that can be annoying and frustrating to classmates, even when they know the behavior is not intentional. Teachers in an inclusion class must learn to anticipate problem behavior before it escalates and involves other students. One of several techniques is known as "antiseptic bouncing." In the case of the Tourette student, as distracting behavior becomes noticeable, the teacher takes nonstigmatizing actions to temporarily separate either the student or other affected classmates from one another so that the behavior ceases to be an issue. This allows the student to calm down, avoid embarrassment, and return to work. For example, the teacher might create an errand, sending the student to the library or main office. Since the behavior is predictable, the teacher can also involve other members of the staff, such as a librarian, who would be prepared to help the student and know when it is appropriate to return to class (Carr et al., 1994).

Phase 3-D is skill development. Even with positive feelings and a clear understanding of the differences among students, they still need to develop specific skills that allow them to communicate and interact. The student with Asperger syndrome may need to be taught how much distance to keep between himself and someone he is speaking to; the general education student may need to develop the ability to substitute literal speaking patterns in place of inventive analogies that her classmate with Asperger syndrome cannot comprehend. These skills need to be deliberately taught by both the special education and general education teachers. Simply encouraging students to talk to one another cannot generally overcome the differences in their styles of thinking and behavior, but teacher-guided opportunities for students to work together on a mathematics problem may help to make the unfamiliar familiar.

Flexible grouping is another way teachers can facilitate including students with special needs in the general education classroom and increase understanding of mathematical concepts. In one model the teacher can start the day's lesson with whole-group instruction and then, partway through, divide the class into groups of four to complete guided practice or to discuss a problem. When this is finished, the group reports out the solution to the class. Each member of the group can be given a task—problem reader, scribe, discussion facilitator, or reporter—based on his or her abilities. Classroom management suggestions include two rules discussed with the class before beginning the flexible grouping session. The first is "Use 6-inch voices," meaning that students should speak at a level so that their voices can only be heard 6 inches away. The second rule is "Ask three before me." That is, if students need assistance and the teacher is helping other students, they should ask three students before asking the teacher. While this may not be appropriate for every lesson, there is much to say about the benefits of focused discourse to develop the deeper understandings needed to achieve the high benchmarks set by the CCSS for mathematics.

These approaches can be helpful guidelines as team teachers prepare for their class in mathematics, but they should not be used as a rulebook for every inclusion class. The most important aspect of inclusion is an awareness that each child is unique in areas that must be understood before learning can take place. These unique strengths and challenges are the driving force behind a successful inclusion program. On the other hand, the differences among students are not haphazard; they form a continuum that can provide guidance in meeting their individual needs, while still managing an entire class of students.

The most familiar continuum of disabilities is the autism spectrum (National Institute of Mental Health, 2013), which aligns pervasive developmental disorders from the most severe conditions, where speech and other communication are all but absent, to the highest functioning "savant genius," who may demonstrate specific intelligences measuring in the superior range, but with social perception in the lowest percentile of the population. Other diagnosed conditions can form similar spectra. This understanding can be a great help to team teachers as they diagnose the learning needs of individual students, so long as they remain acutely aware that each child will present special aspects of need and ability and respond to his or her performance in school accordingly. As the skills to differentiate instruction based on student needs develop, teachers may find that the benefits extend to general education students also.

Thanksgiving Party! A Tier 1 Lesson Guided by the Common Core State Standards

This Tier 1 sixth-grade lesson takes the students on an adventure to solve a problem with multiple solutions guided by CCSS: Math.6.G.1:

> Find the area of right triangles, other triangles, special quadrilaterals, and polygons by composing into rectangles or decomposing into triangles and other shapes; apply these techniques in the context of solving real-world and mathematical problems.

The teacher may wish to watch a video describing the lesson Table for 22, found at www.teachingchannel.org/videos/real-world-geometry-lesson?resume=0, before introducing it to the class. This video describes the standards for mathematical practice used in the lesson and then models the lesson plan.

The problem described is to create a dining table for Thanksgiving that will seat 22 people. Each student receives a 3-foot strip of poster paper that represents the space needed at the table for each seat. Students are asked to create a table with the largest area and a table with the smallest area. After discussing strategies in small groups, the class discusses individual solutions that each group created. The class then comes to consensus on a strategy to solve both problems. Students then create tables by laying their poster strips on the floor to outline the perimeter of the tables. The areas of both tables are calculated, then using inquiry questions the teacher leads the class to some conclusions about the relationship between the perimeter and area of a rectangle.

Teaching Mathematics in Tier 2 and Tier 3 Inclusion Settings

THE TIER 2 SETTING

Tier 2 interventions use systematic, explicit methods in small-group settings. You may recall from previous chapters, skills and concepts begin with the most simple, moving to the more complex, as in every level of RTI, and are driven by ongoing assessment results. Interventions include

- teacher modeling,
- teacher-guided student practice,
- peer-to-peer support, and
- student independent practice with frequent feedback.

Tier 2 interventions should differ from Tier 1 in several aspects:

- additional time beyond regular classroom instruction
- different research-based instructional strategies
- focus on small-group instruction
- different materials

As mentioned in Chapter 3, Diane Bryant led a team of researchers in a study of Tier 2 interventions for a group of first and second graders identified as having difficulties in mathematics (Bryant, Bryant, Gersten, Scammacca, & Chavetz, 2008). They reached several conclusions that can support the work of introducing Tier 2 into an inclusion mathematics program:

1. "Time for Tier 2 intervention is the number one challenge, followed closely by what to do with the other students while secondary interventions are taking place" (p. 61). Schools must design schedules that allow teachers to integrate small-group work into the core curriculum and classwork.

The use of "extra hands," if possible—redirecting the use of school assistants, volunteers, and perhaps a parent group—may help the teacher in implementing Tier 2 instruction with a small group of students in his or her class. Logistics is critical to Tier 2 and, even more so, in Tier 3 instruction. Without careful planning, failure is virtually guaranteed.

2. Tier 2 small-group sessions should be at least 20 minutes in length for 4 days each week in addition to regular instruction. This is a significant investment of time, which again calls for considerable planning by both the teachers and those designing school schedules. Also, planners should recall that many students with difficulty in mathematics also require additional support in reading, which may require Tier 2 intervention in that area as well. (Many, but not all, difficulties in mathematics stem from a struggle with reading comprehension.)

3. Across all grades, but particularly in the lower grades, the most important skills to be developed are basic numbers (understanding place value), fluency with operations (addition, subtraction, multiplication, division), and word problems (translating language into mathematical concepts and mathematical concepts into approaches to a solution). Tier 2 students derive significant benefit from—and in many cases depend on—the personal focus they receive in Tier 2 small-group instruction, provided it is focused on their individual responses to the instruction, and not simply taught according to a prescribed formula. This is consistent with the CCSS focus on the progressions of deep understanding in the content strands of the standards. The Institute for Mathematics Education at the University of Arizona has developed a website with resources on the progression of understandings: http://ime.math.arizona.edu/progressions.

4. The most effective approaches to Tier 2 instruction are explicit, systematic, strategic, and repetitive (Kroesbergen & Van Luit, 2003). This is particularly the case for at-risk students. In their research, Bryant and her colleagues found that multiple, progressive forms of representation (the concrete-semiconcrete-abstract, known as CSA) are especially effective at developing conceptual understanding in Tier 2 settings.

Effective Tier 2 instruction in mathematics focuses on the unique needs of each student and, even more challenging, offers a wide number and range of interventions that give students opportunities to learn the concepts behind simple mathematical procedures and, based on this, to develop and practice specific mathematical skills and deeper understandings. The Common Core State Standards advocate fluency in mathematical computations. During Tier 2 instruction some time should be spent developing fluency, as these skills will scaffold the understanding of more complex mathematics.

This calls for a significant increase in supplemental interventions, compared with any previous period, which would not have been possible without the Internet as a resource. One of the emerging skills of teaching and supervision is the ability to sift through literally thousands of possible programs and activities available online, most of them free of charge, and select those most likely to be effective with specific students. Teachers need to become familiar with websites that recommend the interventions appropriate for their particular students.

One of the most comprehensive is the RTI Action Network's website on mathematics instruction in Tiers 2 and 3 (www.rtinetwork.org/learn/what/rtiandmath). Dozens of research-tested programs are recommended here and on the many other professional mathematics websites. An example of a Tier 2 lesson follows. This lesson plan should be implemented with students in pairs so they can work together and discuss possible solutions with each other. Manipulatives can be used to scaffold students' thinking about the problem. To start the lesson, teachers also may wish to show a short video on CCSS Mathematical Practice Standard 1: Perseverance called Don't Give Up! (www.teachingchannel.org/videos/math-practice-standard-perseverance?fd=1). Teachers may also wish to ask students to name their favorite animal and modify the lesson to include that animal. Personalizing instruction to students' interests may be important for learning mathematics (Ensign, 1997).

TIER 2 LESSON FOR AN INCLUSION CLASS

CCSS 4.MD3 Apply the area and perimeter formulas for rectangles in real world and mathematical problems.

You have just returned from a safari in Kenya, where you saw many beautiful giraffes, lions, zebras, and leopards. Unfortunately one of the zebras was bitten by a lion and ran away before he could be hurt anymore. The zebra needs to be taken to a veterinarian, but because she lives in the bush, there is not one nearby. You decide to take the zebra home, get medical treatment for her, and keep her as a pet. The zebra is a wild animal and is used to roaming in large fields. You need to design an enclosure for your zebra with an area of $280m^2$. You need to consider how you will make the zebra feel at home in your enclosure. What shape will the enclosure be? What other features need to be included in the enclosure to make the zebra comfortable? Your assignment is to draw two possible enclosures including the measurements. Decide which enclosure you think would be most suitable for your zebra, and explain your reasoning.

Today, teachers must develop and use professional judgment as they review the many options available and select those that have the greatest

Figure 7.4   My Pet Zebra

Source: U.S. Fish and Wildlife Service.

potential to help the individual students in their care. They must then be constantly alert to evaluating the success of each selection on their students and make adjustments by introducing alternative approaches when the evidence calls for it. Tier 2 mathematics, particularly in an inclusive setting, represents a new paradigm of professional practice compared with previous generations, when teachers were expected to learn the few mathematics programs approved by their district and apply these to all their students.

THE TIER 3 SETTING

Tier 3 intervention is the most intensive stage within RTI. It is focused on individual students and its components must include instruction in evidence-based curricula, implementation of interventions with fidelity to the RTI process, and analysis of outcomes using formative and summative assessment data. Particularly in inclusive settings, with students whose program is determined by an IEP, it is recommended that individual intervention be administered by a professional with advanced training in the student's particular disability. In some cases, this may be the special education teacher. However, it is critical that individual instruction be based on a professional understanding of the child's disability and responsiveness to specific forms of intervention.

As in Tier 2, instruction during this intervention should be explicit and systematic (Gersten, Beckman et al., 2009). These interventions should include

- models of proficient problem solving,
- verbalization of thought processes,
- guided practice,
- corrective feedback, and
- frequent cumulative review.

They should also emphasize approaches to solving word problems based on common underlying structures, such as recognizing similar patterns and forms of representation.

Tier 3 interventions should always start with the results of the work begun in Tier 2 so there is a smooth and consistent transition. Based on the data collected by progress monitoring in Tier 2, the new work should be individualized to the particular student's challenges with the mathematical topic or standard addressed.

A Note on Inclusion for Talented and Gifted and "Twice-Exceptional" Students

Two of the most overlooked and underserved groups of students are those whose talents and intellectual capabilities would normally be seen as enviable tickets to success in life. Beginning with the National Defense Education Act of 1958 (a crisis-response to the Soviet launch of Sputnik a year earlier), federal money encouraged schools to test and identify students with scores above 130 on standardized IQ tests. The approach was to isolate the "best and the brightest" from the more typical student body, provide a challenging educational experience that would bring forth their maximum potential, and produce the social and intellectual leaders needed to prevail in the Cold War. The areas of talent most in demand were, of course, science and mathematics. During the 1960s and 1970s, separation from the general education population became the sign of an effective talented and gifted program.

By the 1980s, *A Nation at Risk* shifted the attention of policy makers. Instead of developing the most talented of America's students, the new goal was to reverse what the report famously called "a rising tide of mediocrity" (U.S. National Commission on Excellence in Education, 1983, p. 1). The threat from global competition changed the focus of education from encouraging the brightest individuals to improving the masses of underperforming students.

During these same years, the rise of special education, with its support for the most challenged students, led to even greater separation of students according to levels of intellectual performance. Attention shifted away from both the highest performing students and the most challenged, and became focused on the mediocre performance of general education. Exceptional students experienced new levels of relative isolation from their general education peers.

Compounding the problem of isolation, since the late 1970s yet another group of students became recognized. These are the ones who demonstrate the qualities of *both* the special needs and gifted populations but—perhaps not surprisingly—could not be appropriately served by the resources available to either (Maker, 1977). This group became known as "twice exceptional" students: individuals who were intellectually gifted but also met the criteria for certification in special education. They became more widely recognized after the 1990s, as large numbers of students with high-functioning autism and Asperger syndrome were identified and diagnosed for the first time. As with special education and gifted students, the twice-exceptionals were initially educated in relative isolation from the general education population.

As schools prepare for an inclusion program, supervisors and administrators need to be aware of how widely the net now needs to be cast. The list of previously overlooked groups of students includes not only the "classic" special education population, but also the talented and gifted, the twice exceptional, English language learners, and all others who may be part of a particular school or district.

In certain schools, the educational and administrative challenges of bringing all these students together into a single learning environment can seem overwhelming, particularly to the individual classroom teacher. Without effective training and collaboration, a general education mathematics teacher who confronts a class containing a mixture of special needs, talented and gifted, twice exceptional, and/or English language learners is almost certain to feel abandoned and unable to teach. The most effective response to this challenge is in the approaches described in this chapter:

- *Collegial and team teaching*, in which professionals from multiple areas of expertise pool their talents to design an individualized program for each student.
- *Professional development* that is intensive and continual. The skills of teachers, supervisors, and administrators need to be constantly renewed so that they can be prepared for the challenges that are certain to arise in any effective inclusion program.

As we have said previously, the transition from the traditional, 20th century model of education to Common Core State Standards, Response to Intervention, and inclusive schooling represents nothing less than a paradigm shift in the way teachers teach and children learn. After more than a generation of scattered, localized attempts at reform, these initiatives now carry the full weight of national commitment, funding, and in many cases, federal law.

Professionals who leave familiar expectations (homogeneous group instruction) and enter new surroundings (inclusive, individualized instruction) can succeed only if their mind-set is attuned to a spirit of learning and discovery, rather than assurances and predictability. This is probably the most valuable insight that teachers and administrators can develop as they accept the challenges presented to schools today. Problems of scheduling; individualization; professional coordination; limitations of time, funding, and resources; and a host of others can seem intractable within the framework of traditional school organization. But, in the words of Joel Barker (2001), "What may be impossible to do in the old paradigm may be easy to do in the new paradigm" (p. 11). To make this happen, the shift from group to individualized learning, and from homogeneous to inclusive classes, will call for a change of orientation that leads to new forms of interaction on the part of every member of a school's educational team: teachers, supervisors, and administrators.

Summary

Teaching mathematics to an inclusion class so all students have an equal chance to reach the benchmarks set by the Common Core State Standards presents special challenges for the mathematics teacher. In most cases, some form of team teaching is required to ensure that academic standards for mathematics are met at the same time that the work is appropriately modified for each student's unique needs and, when necessary, the requirements of an IEP. Before the mathematics and modifications, the teacher must first prepare students who come with a wide variety of needs to understand and eventually value their differences. In addition to general techniques for sensitivity training that would be appropriate for a class in any academic subject, mathematics teachers need to tailor their teaching in ways that include the Common Core academic content, the RTI instructional framework, and a deep awareness of the differences among students. Understanding this, Tier 2 and Tier 3 instruction presents special opportunities and challenges.

 Tech Byte

R T I   A C T I O N   N E T W O R K

www.rtinetwork.org

The most comprehensive, accessible, and useful site for mathematics teachers working in inclusion programs is the RTI Action Network (www .rtinetwork.org). It contains pages titled Tier 1—Core Instruction, Tier 2—Group Interventions, and Tier 3—Intensive Interventions, with additional sections focused on appropriate work for Pre-K, K–5, middle school, and high school curricula.

Teachers can use the site for a comprehensive discussion of the principles underlying inclusion within an RTI framework and find numerous specific examples of interventions for each of the tiers at all grade levels. Video clips, discussions, and expert commentary are available. Figures 7.5, 7.6, and 7.7 present the RTI Action Network home pages for Tiers 1, 2, and 3.

Figure 7.5   RTI Action Network: Tier 1

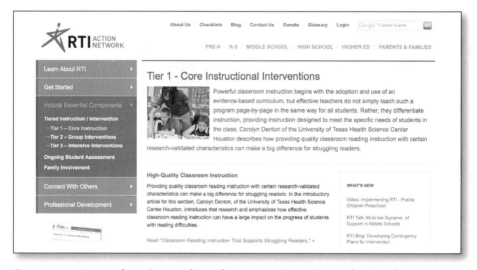

Source: www.rtinetwork.org/essential/tieredinstruction/tier1. Copyright 2013 by RTI Action Network, a program of National Center for Learning Disabilities, Inc. All rights reserved. Reprinted with permission. For more information, visit www.RTINetwork.org.

Figure 7.6   RTI Action Network: Tier 2

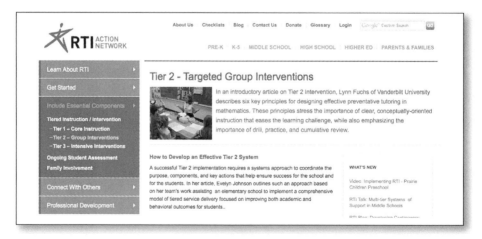

Source: www.rtinetwork.org/essential/tieredinstruction/tier2. Copyright 2013 by RTI Action Network, a program of National Center for Learning Disabilities, Inc. All rights reserved. Reprinted with permission. For more information, visit www.RTINetwork.org.

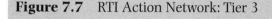

Figure 7.7 RTI Action Network: Tier 3

Source: www.rtinetwork.org/essential/tieredinstruction/tier3. Copyright 2013 by RTI Action Network, a program of National Center for Learning Disabilities, Inc. All rights reserved. Reprinted with permission. For more information, visit www.RTINetwork.org.

Resources for Future Study

Examples of Effective RtI Use and Decision Making: Part 3—Mathematics

http://rtinetwork.org/essential/assessment/data-based/examples-of-effective-rti-use-and-decision-making-part-3-mathematics

This website concludes a three-part series of articles with case examples in mathematics to show how RTI decisions are reached in real-world scenarios. For each case example, a series of three questions that should be asked is provided. The questions addressed in this case study are: Is there a gradewide learning problem? Is there a classwide or individual learning problem? Did intervention successfully resolve the problem?

Why RTI Works for Sanger

www.rtinetwork.org/voices-archives/entry/2/150

This article describes an RTI inclusion mathematics and reading project for 10,500 students in Sanger School District, in Fresno County, California. In this district, over 76% of students are eligible for free or reduced-price lunch and 25% are English language learners. After this initiative, Sanger had 48% of students with disabilities score proficient in mathematics, while the state had 34.5% of students with disabilities and 28% of schools with a similar poverty score proficient.

Sorting and Classifying Equations Overview
Video, Grade 8, Math, Collaboration

www.teachingchannel.org/videos/sorting-classifying-equations-overview?fd=1#

This approximately 10-minute video describes a lesson on equations guided by the Common Core State Standard Math.8.EE.7a:

> Give examples of linear equations in one variable with one solution, infinitely many solutions, or no solutions. Show which of these possibilities is the case by successively transforming the given equation into simpler forms, until an equivalent equation of the form $x = a$, $a = a$, or $a = b$ results (where a and b are different numbers).

Instructional Strategies: Teaching Mathematics

www.ldonline.org/educators/strategies/math

The site contains the following five articles that provide information on how to teach mathematics to students with learning disabilities, including dyscalcula, a specific math learning disability:

- Components of Effective Mathematics Instruction
- 10 Tips for Software Selection for Math Instruction
- Number Sense: Rethinking Arithmetic Instruction for Students With Mathematical Disabilities
- Students With Nonverbal Learning Disabilities
- Technology-Supported Math Instruction for Students With Disabilities: Two Decades of Research and Development

Glossary

Inclusion (as a service delivery model): Students with identified disabilities are educated with general education age-/grade-level peers.

8

The Role of Parents Helping Students to Achieve

John Kappenberg and Helene Fallon

Seek first to understand, then to be understood.

—Stephen R. Covey (1989, p. 235)

In this chapter you will learn:

- The distinctions between client and consultant relationships among parents and teachers
- The foundations and uses of a consultant relationship in the area of mathematics, Response to Intervention (RTI), and Common Core State Standards
- Specific techniques that teachers can use to develop a productive relationship with parents that will help students achieve the benchmarks set by the Common Core
- Online resources that can support teachers in developing productive relationships with parents and parents in staying informed about the Common Core for mathematics and RTI

Sue Lui is a seventh grader who lives with her father, Kim. Mr. Lui is meeting with Sue's mathematics teacher, Satasha Thompson. Sue attended the district's elementary school from prekindergarten through fifth grade and has been a student in the middle school starting with the sixth grade.

Ms. Thompson believes that Sue started the year with a negative attitude toward mathematics. Her sixth-grade report indicates that she was quiet and cooperative, but beginning in February of her seventh-grade year, she has been referred to the office several times for disciplinary issues. Ms. Thompson has noted that January is the time that her school's curriculum, which is guided by the Common Core State Standards, called for the class to begin the topics of factoring, equivalent expressions, and probability.

Sue began refusing to complete classroom assignments and would spend much of the class time with her head on the desk. When Ms. Thompson asked Sue to pay attention, she become confrontational. She refused to complete either classroom or homework assignments.

Since the first grade, Sue has been a B student in English and social studies but marginal in science and mathematics. She attended afterschool tutoring classes for mathematics in the second and third grades but nothing since then. In spite of several requests from Ms. Thompson, she refuses to come for tutoring in mathematics either before or after school.

Kim Lui is a single working father and has come to meet with Ms. Thompson.

Virtually everyone involved with schools agrees, at least in public, that parent involvement is critical to every child's academic success (Lent, Brown, & Hackett, 2000). Over the years, a consistent 85% of the public reports that they believe parents are essential to the educational process (Mitchell, 2008; Rose, Gallup, & Elam, 1997). In private, many professionals would limit that involvement primarily to supporting their school's program actively and, preferably, without question (Roberts, 2012). Others recognize the potential of parent input to add unique perspective and information on their students' capabilities and needs. In short, the range of opinion among educators about the role that parents ought to play in the school's educational process has never been more diverse (Burton & Kappenberg, 2012).

Regardless of anyone's personal disposition on the role of parents in the school curriculum, when the No Child Left Behind Act (2001) became law, school professionals and parents had to adapt to a new federally mandated relationship. The law called for parents to be "actively" involved and "equal partners" in decision-making processes that affected their child's educational program (Public Law 107-110, 20 U.S.C.A. 6301 et. seq. Section 1112; 1114 (b) (2); 1116; 1118 (a) (1) (2), (b) (2), (b) (2)-(4), (e)).

It is difficult to argue against parent involvement in decisions that impact their child. It is even more difficult to agree on exactly what this involvement would look like in an actual meeting between, for example, the parent of a seventh-grade student and her teacher as they discuss the parent's concerns with how solving problems involving area, surface area, and volume is being taught. This new relationship opens an array of challenges for the mathematics teacher who is faced with new regulations governing both the Common Core State Standards that guide instruction and the involvement of parents in academic decision making for their child.

The paradigm for parent involvement in American schools has been in place for generations: Teachers provide the education and parents support the teachers (Dodd & Konzal, 2000). We see examples of this wherever we search for general information on parent involvement. The masthead for a parent-centered website highlights the theme: "Successful parent involvement programs provide the link between the home and school that are essential to the growth and development of children, and enable principals, teachers and parents to work together towards a shared mission on behalf of learners" (Lewis, 1996). Meador (2013) offered six points of advice to help parents support their child in school:

1. Be supportive—voice your support actively.

2. Be involved and stay involved—keep up with the work your child is given.

3. Don't bad-mouth the teacher in front of your child.

4. Follow through—back up actions of teachers and administrators at home.

5. Don't take the child's word for the truth—assume the teacher and parent are on the same team, rather than adversaries.

6. Don't make excuses for your child—don't blame teachers when the child becomes frustrated with work or with school.

These represent the traditional understanding of what schools expect from parents: support, follow-through at home, a team relationship between parent and school, with the school setting the agenda and parents helping to carry it out. This model has, in fact, represented a core value in American culture, but it is one that the new laws governing parent involvement are attempting to steer in a new direction.

Most important, teachers need to help parents enter the conversation with a knowledge base of the instructional strategies and content taught in their child's school, which are different from the content or instructional strategies in place when the parents went to school. The resources at the end of this chapter provide a starting point for these conversations.

The meeting between Ms. Thompson, the mathematics teacher, and Mr. Lui, the parent, is not going well. Ms. Thompson began by describing Sue's growing disinterest in her classwork and homework and the recent disciplinary problems. She then discusses the importance of mathematics grades to the child's high school record and the fact that the new Common Core State Standards are forcing every student to meet new benchmarks and develop deep understandings in all the areas covered in the seventh grade.

Mr. Lui then talks about how he has become increasingly upset over his daughter's reaction to the seventh-grade mathematics program. He tells Ms. Thompson that, since January, Sue doesn't like going to school and hates the work in factoring and probability. She used to like geometry but has no interest in anything related to mathematics if she can't draw pictures of it. Besides, Mr. Lui says, "Sue can't understand what she's ever going to do with this stuff." He adds, "Why do these kids have to spend so much time on things that are so abstract and have no connection to anything they're going to do once they get out of school?"

Ms. Thompson tries to convince Sue's father that the seventh-grade curriculum driven by the Common Core State Standards for mathematics has been through rigorous national review, has been adopted by over 45 states, and that mastery is required for Sue's graduation. "Sue just needs a little more time to get used to the new material," she tells Mr. Lui. "We've seen dozens of students go through problems like this and eventually they learn how to handle it. I'm sure this is just normal adolescent independence and in a few more weeks she'll be back on track."

The Client Model of Parent-Professional Relationship

In a previous publication (Burton & Kappenberg, 2012), we described the traditional view of parent involvement as a client model and contrasted it with a consultant model, more attuned to the goals of the new laws governing parent involvement in schools. The traditional relationship between schools and parents is a variation of that between schools and students, or parent and child: a hierarchy based on natural authority, in this case, the authority of professionals who possess educational expertise over lay people, who do not. The relationship is inherently unequal (Tiegerman-Farber & Radziewicz, 1997). "Although all schools routinely invite parents to attend informational meetings and conferences, few invite them to actively participate in extended and engaging activities" (Dodd & Konzal, 2000, p. 11).

Consider how the conversation would have been different if the parent had an understanding of the curriculum after the teacher provided him with information on the Common Core in a collaborative way, or showed him one or two websites that demonstrate lesson plans for one of these critical areas. For example, the National Council of Teachers of Mathematics has a number of lesson plans aligned with the Common Core State Standards. For the Grade 7 critical area of focus (*Developing understanding of and applying proportional relationships*) the lesson Feeding Frenzy (http://illuminations.nctm .org/LessonDetail.aspx?id=L781) provides opportunities for students to think critically about a real-world application: a baking problem. In this lesson, students multiply and divide a recipe to feed groups of various sizes using unit rates or proportions.

The conversation in Table 8.1 illustrates the client-based relationship between Ms. Thompson and Mr. Lui in more detail.

To be an equal partner in the academic success of the child, the parent needs the resources to be able to "speak the same language" as the teacher. Numerous websites, such as www.corestandards.org/assets/CCSSI_ Math%20Standards.pdf, can help the parent and teacher better understand the academic focus of the curriculum and facilitate a more equal conversation. Table 8.2 describes the four critical areas that instructional time should focus on in the Grade 7 curriculum guided by the Common Core.

This and other resources can be a good beginning to develop a better parent-teacher relationship. To take advantage of these tools, both the teacher and parent need to cultivate a new perspective on the role that parents can play in their child's education. Schools need to provide opportunities for parents to become aware of resources which may be helpful to them. Sometimes this can be as simple and inexpensive as providing these resources on the school website or enlisting the support of parent-teacher organizations or others in the educational community.

The Impact of RTI, Common Core, and Parent Involvement Regulations on the Client Model

We have stressed that, in a school's instructional program, RTI is a framework without content. It provides a method for diagnosing student needs and evaluating how effective instruction is with individual students, but it does not contain the actual content of instruction. It is an example of the scientific method applied to the field of instruction. The problem-solving

Table 8.1   Conversation Between Parent and Mathematics Teacher Based on a Client Relationship

Parent:	I'm really upset with the way Sue is reacting to the math work you've been giving her since January. I don't know what the problem is, but all of a sudden she can't understand anything that's going on and I can't do anything to help her. I don't remember anything about factoring from high school and I never learned anything about probability. What's a parent supposed to do? And why does she have to do this kind of work anyway?
Teacher:	You've probably heard about the Common Core State Standards which guides our curriculum in mathematics. It's part of a nationwide change in the way we will be teaching; the curriculum we're covering is all part of these new state requirements. Unfortunately, there is not much room for us to make changes. We're all trying to adapt to it.
Parent:	That's all I'm hearing—that's all anyone is talking about—"Common Core, Common Core." Don't you people have any say in what you're teaching these kids?
Teacher:	Actually, I think the material in the new curriculum is a lot better than it used to be. And more important, it makes sense that everyone across the country will be covering the same content so that, when Sue graduates, her grades in math will mean something to colleges and employers. It may be difficult now, but in the long run, she'll be better off.
Parent:	But she just can't understand the work she's doing now—she can't draw pictures of it, the way she did with the geometry. She can't even draw number lines.
Teacher:	One of the things that we learn from math is to move beyond the kind of thinking we're comfortable with and into areas that are more difficult. This is the kind of work that the job market is calling for, and at some point Sue is going to have to learn it. I'm sorry we can't make it easier but, again, it's something that will be a big benefit for her if she can just start to understand that.
Parent:	So what am I supposed to do to help? I either don't remember most of this work from my own high school years or, when it comes to problems on factoring and probability, I've never even heard of them.
Teacher:	You're not expected to be an expert in math—that's what we're here for. I've asked Sue to come for extra help mornings or afternoons, but she hasn't shown up. It would be a big help if you would give me some support and insist that she come. That's one of the most important things that parents can do to help their children.

Table 8.2   Critical Areas of Understanding in Grade 7 Mathematics Curriculum Guided by the Common Core State Standards

1. Developing understanding of and applying proportional relationships

Students extend their understanding of ratios and develop understanding of proportionality to solve single- and multi-step problems. Students use their understanding of ratios and proportionality to solve a wide variety of percent problems, including those involving discounts, interest, taxes, tips, and percent increase or decrease. Students solve problems about scale drawings by relating corresponding lengths between the objects or by using the fact that relationships of lengths within an object are preserved in similar objects. Students graph proportional relationships and understand the unit rate informally as a measure of the steepness of the related line, called the slope. They distinguish proportional relationships from other relationships.

2. Developing understanding of operations with rational numbers and working with expressions and linear equations

Students develop a unified understanding of number, recognizing fractions, decimals (that have a finite or a repeating decimal representation), and percents as different representations of rational numbers. Students extend addition, subtraction, multiplication, and division to all rational numbers, maintaining the properties of operations and the relationships between addition and subtraction, and multiplication and division. By applying these properties, and by viewing negative numbers in terms of everyday contexts (e.g., amounts owed or temperatures below zero), students explain and interpret the rules for adding, subtracting, multiplying, and dividing with negative numbers. They use the arithmetic of rational numbers as they formulate expressions and equations in one variable and use these equations to solve problems.

3. Solving problems involving scale drawings and informal geometric constructions, and working with two- and three-dimensional shapes to solve problems involving area, surface area, and volume

Students continue their work with area from Grade 6, solving problems involving the area and circumference of a circle and surface area of three-dimensional objects. In preparation for work on congruence and similarity in Grade 8 they reason about relationships among two-dimensional figures using scale drawings and informal geometric constructions, and they gain familiarity with the relationships between angles formed by intersecting lines. Students work with three-dimensional figures, relating them to two-dimensional figures by examining cross-sections.

(Continued)

Table 8.2 (Continued)

They solve real-world and mathematical problems involving area, surface area, and volume of two- and three-dimensional objects composed of triangles, quadrilaterals, polygons, cubes and right prisms.

4. Drawing inferences about populations based on samples

Students build on their previous work with single data distributions to compare two data distributions and address questions about differences between populations. They begin informal work with random sampling to generate data sets and learn about the importance of representative samples for drawing inferences.

Source: Council of Chief State School Officers (2010, p. 46). © Copyright 2010. National Governors Association Center for Best Practices and Council of Chief State School Officers. All rights reserved.

methodology of RTI derives from the scientific method and includes four basic steps: (1) problem identification and definition, (2) problem analysis, (3) intervention plan development and implementation, and (4) evaluation of the plan's effectiveness" (Clark & Tilly, 2010, p. 15). As the name implies, it is focused on students' response to instructional interventions, tracked by progress monitoring, (see Chapter 4), but does not provide the interventions themselves.

RTI provides process guidelines while the Common Core sets the standards and academic content for mathematics instruction. But neither can offer the teacher guidance on exactly how to present the academic content to a class or adapt the presentation to individual students (Kendall, 2011). For this, the teacher needs insight, and often inspiration, from some other source. For new teachers, the source may be readings in lesson planning or help from colleagues; for veteran teachers, years of experience can add a wealth of resources and options. But for any teacher, one of the most productive resources for ideas on how to understand and respond to the difficulties faced by individual students is their parents.

The Consultant Model of Parent-Professional Relationship

RTI requires access to every possible idea and all relevant information in responding to the needs of an individual child. In most cases, the professional expertise and experience of the staff do not include the full range of insights needed to respond to a distinct challenge that a student presents. Thus, the insight and input of the parents make up a source of expertise that the professionals cannot afford to miss.

Compared with traditional instruction, RTI and the Common Core call for a vast resource of alternative interventions available to the teacher from without, and a new demand for insight and creativity from within. In the past, instruction was largely about finding ways of bringing every student in a class into a single learning experience. A single plan covered the group, and deviation from the plan was considered generally unacceptable. Under these conditions, the role of the teacher in relation to the parent was similar to the role of the parent in relation to the child: provide caring guidance based on expertise and expect cooperation and support in return.

In an RTI and Common Core–based program, where the premium is on adapting the instructional aspects of the program (the interventions) to the students, one of the most critical requirements becomes insight into the needs of these individual students. Under these conditions, it becomes clear that parents need to be—and are capable of—providing much more than simply support for the expertise of the teacher. They must be seen as an invaluable source of insight into the needs of their children, not as just supporting members of the instructional team.

Since professionals depend more than ever on information, resources, and ideas about *students* as well as instruction, they need to broaden the scope of their expertise. Their traditional hierarchical relationship with parents needs to be reexamined. Parent involvement should move beyond the client model, with parents supporting programs the schools have designed. Teachers, administrators, and supervisors need to value and utilize parents as an essential resource in understanding the needs of individual students, with specialized knowledge of the students' capabilities and learning needs, and an expertise that cannot be found elsewhere. Rather than passive clients, parents need to be seen as actively contributing consultants. They are not educational professionals, but they are in a position to contribute unique, specialized, and essential insights to the teacher's understanding of individual students. Peggy Lou Morgan (2009) told parents, "You have become the expert on your child. You know what his behavior means, and you automatically respond in the appropriate way" (p. 3). Parents are usually the only people who have interacted with the child over a long period of time, across multiple environments and transitions that the child has faced. When teachers focus their instruction on individual students, this expertise can be a critical element in their own professional practice.

In this new process, a parent-professional conversation might probe the parent's experience with the child, actions he or she has taken in the past, outcomes of those actions, the reasons for the parent's interpretation of the child's behavior in school and at home, and similar questions, looking for insights aimed at discovering the most effective intervention when previous efforts have failed. Again, the parent is not just cooperating or supporting, but is contributing invaluable resources. Table 8.3 illustrates the contrast between client and consultant relationships.

Table 8.3   Client vs. Consultant Relationships

	Client Relationship	*Consultant Relationship*
Expertise	**The professional** has specialized academic training in education. **The parent** is usually without academic training in education.	**The professional** has specialized academic training in education. **The parent** has intensive knowledge gained from "field experience" working with the child.
Agenda	**The professional** sets the educational agenda for the child, based on professional judgment within the mandates of school and state educational standards. **The parent** is asked to support the agenda.	**The professional** consults with the parent on how to discover and meet the child's needs within the framework of school and state standards. **The parent,** as consultant, contributes ideas on interventions that might meet both sets of standards.
Assessment	**The professional** reports periodically to the parent on how the interventions are going in school. **The parent** is asked to adjust his or her support for these interventions at home with the child.	**The professional** reports periodically to the parent on how the interventions are going in school. **The parent** reports on how the interventions are going at home. **Both parties** discuss ways of adjusting the intervention and coordinating these adjustments in both venues.

Source: Burton & Kappenberg (2012, p. 140).

The case study of Mr. Lui (the parent) and Ms. Thompson (the teacher) that opened this chapter is an example of a conversation based on the professional-client model. The relationship is hierarchical: The teacher's role is to represent and enforce her school's Common Core program in mathematics, and to do this she tries to win the parent's support. The parent believes that the Common Core is harming his daughter by forcing her to do work that is too abstract and difficult and, worse, has no relation to anything she will ever need later in life. The problems with this relationship become evident when disagreements arise. Table 8.4 presents a conversation that Mr. Lui and Ms. Thompson might have had under a professional-consultant relationship.

Table 8.4   Conversation Between Parent and Mathematics Teacher Based on a Consultant Relationship

Parent:	I'm really upset with the way Sue is reacting to the math work you've been giving her since January. I don't know what the problem is, but all of a sudden she can't understand anything that's going on and I can't do anything to help her. I don't remember anything about factoring from high school, and I never learned anything about probability. What's a parent supposed to do? And why does she have to do this kind of work anyway?
Teacher:	What else can you tell me about Sue's reaction to the new work? Tell me whatever you can about what she says and does at home.
Parent:	She comes home every day screaming that none of it makes sense anymore. You used to be a good teacher but now she can't understand anything you're talking about. She blames it all on this "Common Core" that is all anyone is talking about.
Teacher:	OK, I understand. Does she talk about why factoring is so much of a problem compared with the work we were doing at the beginning of the year?
Parent:	She just says she can't understand it—she can't draw pictures of it, the way she did with the geometry. She can't even draw number lines.
Teacher:	Anything else?
Parent:	This business with probability: It sounds like something that might have some use in the real world, but the problems in the book don't talk about anything except numbers and equal signs and formulas.
Teacher:	You said you weren't able to give her much help at home. Is that because you don't have enough time, or is it the work itself?
Parent:	I have time in the evenings. It's the work that is the problem. Either I don't remember it from my own high school years or I never had it. I don't know anything about math—you're supposed to be the expert in that.
Teacher:	But you're the expert in understanding Sue. I've known her for a few months, and only for an hour a day in math class. You've known her all her life; you know the things that she likes and the things that turn her off. In the long run, these are the things that are going to get her through the math program. Right now you've given me a lot of important ideas about why she doesn't like the work we're doing now. You've told me that she has trouble with anything she can't visualize. That's something I can work with. The textbook we're using doesn't give many concrete illustrations of problems in factoring and probability, but I'm sure I can come up with some, now that I know it might make a difference. Is there anything else you can tell me that might help?

Source: Adapted from Burton & Kappenberg (2012, pp. 141–142).

The teacher has guided the conversation from one of hierarchy and authority (in the original scenario) to consultation and collaboration. Without surrendering control of her program, she recognizes the parent as an "outside expert" whose insights are essential to the child's success. The teacher needs and asks for the parent's perspective; she is also aware that more information will be coming when the outside testing results are known and is prepared to adjust her response at that time.

She recognizes that the parent's perspective and the teacher's perspective are inherently different: Teachers have to consider the needs of all the children in a class and also the requirements of state and district regulations, such as the Common Core; parents are generally concerned about only one thing—the welfare of their own child. Knowing this, Ms. Thompson now avoids defending, or even explaining, the Common Core at this stage of the discussion. She knows that as long as the conversation is focused on Sue, Mr. Lui will likely be open to giving any information that the teacher asks for. After a confident consultant relationship is established, in which both parties respect the expertise of the other, Mr. Lui will be more open to hearing the arguments behind why the district has adopted the Common Core. Habit 5 of Stephen Covey's (1989) *The Seven Habits of Highly Effective People*—seek first to understand, then to be understood—crystalizes the wisdom and necessity of understanding the perspectives of other people before it is possible to engage in any meaningful relationship.

When—and only when—the parent believes that the teacher genuinely understands the parent's concerns, it is possible to talk about what the parent can do to help the child with mathematics. At this point, the conversation between Ms. Thompson and Mr. Lui might continue as depicted in Table 8.5.

Table 8.5   Conversation Between Parent and Mathematics Teacher Based on a Consultant Relationship (continued)

Teacher:	If we can get back to what you were saying about how you can help Sue with the math . . . I think it would help all three of us if we took a look at the Common Core standards themselves. You know, this whole thing is almost as new to those of us teaching math as it is to the kids and the parents. It's designed to raise standards across the country, but that's going to take a lot of getting used to. We're all learning together.
Parent:	What can you tell me?
Teacher:	Why don't we start with one of the things that Sue is having problems with—probability and statistics. Here is the Common Core content for statistics and probability. *[She hands the parent a one-page copy of the seventh-*

grade domain for Statistics and Probability.] Without getting too far into the terminology, there are only three main topics—what they call "clusters"—in seventh-grade statistics. The first is using a small sample from a group of people to learn something important about the entire group, such as when the polls report on how one candidate is doing in an election, compared with another.

> The actual wording of the first standard is "Use random sampling to draw inferences about a population."

The second is to use data to compare two different groups; for example, if we wanted to find out whether more girls are becoming doctors today than 10 years ago.

> The actual wording of the second standard is "Draw informal comparative inferences about two populations."

And the third is to do a better job of predicting things that will happen. All of this is pretty useful stuff.

> The actual wording of the third standard is "Investigate chance processes and develop, use, and evaluate probability models."

Parent: I'd rather have you explain it than have to read it the way it is here.

Teacher: It's just "educationalese." Every field has its own private language—like the fine print in the home mortgage you sign. The important thing is that it means that what Sue is learning is going to make a big difference in how prepared she is to be successful after she leaves school. Things like probability and prediction are a huge part of everyone's life—not just in a job, but in things like deciding which car is more likely to last 10 years and which will have to be turned in after only 4 or 5. The Common Core standards are designed to focus our work on what these kids will actually need, not what mathematicians do.

Parent: Is Sue getting this kind of work now? She keeps saying it's all abstract and she can't visualize anything, the way she used to do with the geometry.

Teacher: That's a good point. I've been trying to keep the work concrete, but sometimes it's easy to spend a little too much time making sure everyone knows the foundation—the formulas and the drills—and not realize that these kids need visuals and concrete things to hold on to. I'm glad you brought this up. We'll have to find some better ways of covering the material next week.

Source: Adapted from Burton & Kappenberg (2012, pp. 141–142).

The teacher developed a consultant relationship with the parent, a relationship in which each has an interdependent role to play. She can now gain valuable insights from the parent, such as the reasons why the student is not open to the work in statistics and probability, and at the same time become a teacher to the parent, helping him understand the rationale behind the

Common Core in general and probability in particular—which will help the parent support and encourage the student at home. At the same time, the parent has given the teacher information about the student that will be essential in helping her move beyond her resistance to the new material. If the process is successful, several outcomes may be expected:

- The parent's distress will be lowered and replaced with a sense of empowerment and involvement in his child's program.
- The teacher will maintain control of her other responsibilities as a professional, that is, to teach all the students in the class and to support the school's investment in the Common Core.
- Most important, the open-minded search for an approach that works for this particular child is likely to produce a far better outcome for her than if the parent and teacher engaged in a power struggle over which one was better prepared to decide what the child needs.

The rest of the chapter will identify and review several of the many resources that are available to parents—and to professionals who are working with parents—to build a consultant, rather than client, relationship.

 Tech Byte

NATIONAL NETWORK OF
PARTNERSHIP SCHOOLS (NNPS)

www.csos.jhu.edu/p2000

The site contains information on improving parent-school collaboration in the following ways:

- Increase knowledge of new concepts and strategies.
- Use research results to develop tools and materials that will improve policy and practice.
- Provide professional development conferences and workshops.
- Share best practices of parental involvement and community connections.
- Recognize excellent partnership programs at the school, district, organization, and state levels.

Its website is a rich resource that can help parents and teachers better understand one another and learn to speak the same language.

In reviewing the relationship between Ms. Thompson, the mathematics teacher, and Mr. Lui, Sue's father, we can see that a website such as NNPS's can help both find common ground within their two separate areas of expertise in helping Sue with her mathematics.

The National Network of Partnership Schools is an example of an invest-ment in stakeholder expertise that we have referred to as the consultant model of parent-professional relationship. It can help teachers better under-stand the insights that parents have into their children's unique needs. But it is also a useful source of support for parents who need to understand the technical areas of mathematics as they try to help their children at home. In the case of Ms. Thompson and Mr. Lui, both can benefit from the extensive resources that the NNPS continually gathers and posts. Teachers gain insight into approaches to parent support that have been successful in other schools, and parents gain new experience in helping their children with mathematics problems that both are struggling with.

Exploring the National Network of Partnership Schools website, we begin on the home page, shown in Figure 8.1.

Here, we find a description of the overall program, representative publica-tions, a survey, references to research, resources for professional development, and contact information. However, the best way to access the full range of the site is to click on the Site Map (circled). The site map is shown in Figure 8.2.

Figure 8.1 National Network of Partnership Schools Home Page

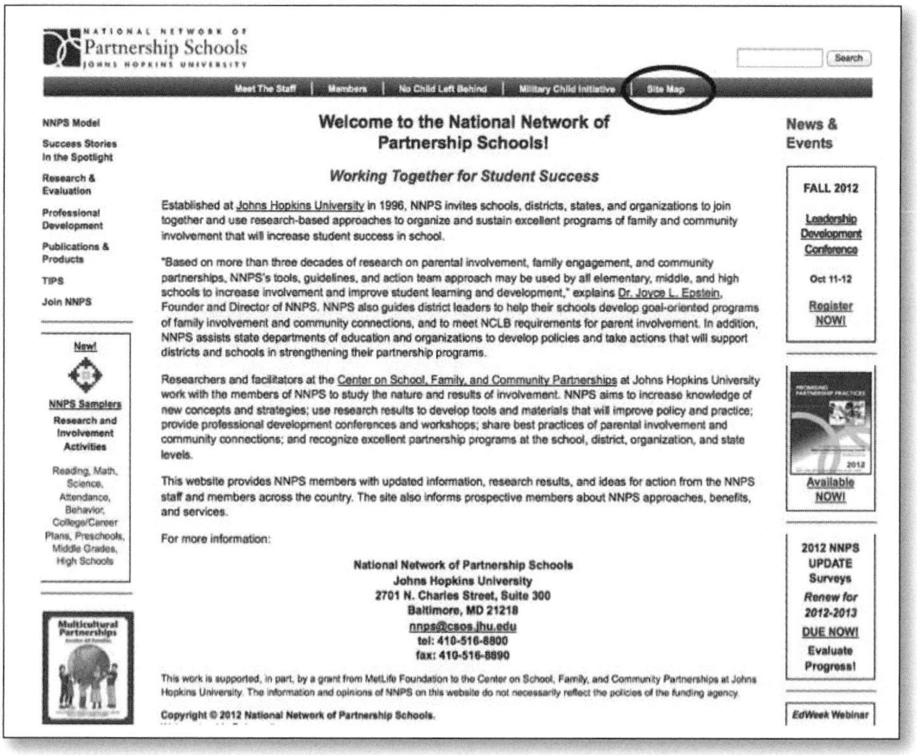

Source: www.csos.jhu.edu/p2000. National Network of Partnership Schools (NNPS) at Johns Hopkins University, www.partnershipschools.org.

Figure 8.2   National Network of Partnership Schools Site Map

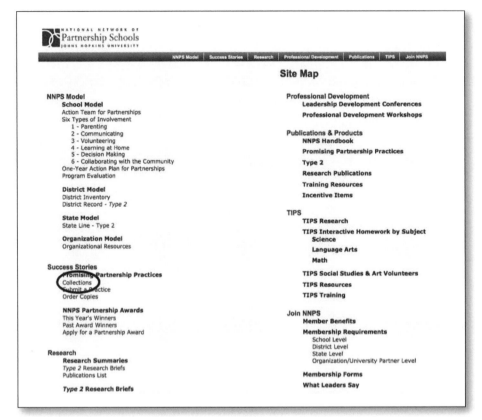

Source: www.csos.jhu.edu/p2000/site.htm. National Network of Partnership Schools (NNPS) at Johns Hopkins University, www.partnershipschools.org.

This lists six forms of parent-teacher involvement—parenting, communicating, volunteering, learning at home, decision making, and collaborating with the community—each with links to ideas, examples, and resources. There is also information focused primarily for professionals: publications and products, professional development, and research. One of the most useful areas for both teachers and parents is under the heading Success Stories. We access the primary site by clicking on Collections (circled). The home page of Collections is shown in Figure 8.3.

The Collections page provides access to examples of promising practices collected under 12 subject areas, including math, and providing access to a collection that dates from 2000 through 2010 (1999 and earlier require a member login). In mathematics alone, this includes more than 70 individual items. We begin by clicking on the most recent date (circle #1) and then selecting Math under the Search menu (circle #2). This takes us to a collection of summaries from the mathematics resources available from 2012, shown on Figure 8.4.

Figure 8.3   National Network of Partnership Schools Collections Page

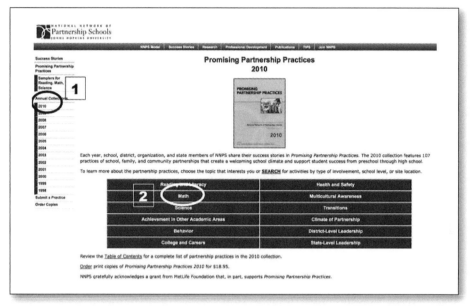

Source: www.csos.jhu.edu/p2000/ppp/2006/index.htm. National Network of Partnership Schools (NNPS) at Johns Hopkins University, www.partnershipschools.org.

Figure 8.4   National Network of Partnership Schools Math Articles Summaries Page

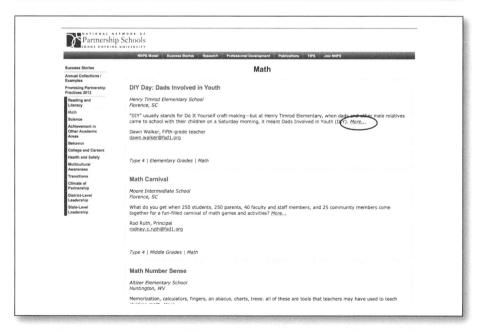

Source: http://www.csos.jhu.edu/p2000/ppp/2012/index.htm. National Network of Partnership Schools (NNPS) at Johns Hopkins University, www.partnershipschools.org.

From the selection of resources, we glance through the brief summaries. We select an article titled "DIY Day: Dads Involved in Youth," since it seems that it might give our parent, Mr. Lui, an idea of how he might help his daughter with the homework that both have trouble understanding. To access the full article, we click on More . . . (circled), which takes us to the resource we are looking for, shown in Figure 8.5.

This particular article focuses on ways that parents across the country are becoming involved in helping their children adjust to the "new math curricula and performance standards" (i.e., the Common Core). It describes a Saturday activity for parents who work with their children to apply the math they learn at school in building birdfeeders and birdhouses according to Common Core standards, using seed donated by a local Lowes store. The program was developed at a school in South Carolina, in which teachers and students "learned math, constructed crafts, and built family-school partnerships."

The story of how this evolved can be a help to both the parent and the teacher. The parent can develop confidence that it is possible to learn enough math to help his daughter—by seeing that other schools have done this— and the teacher can pick up ideas on one approach to helping parents become better at supporting their children.

Resources for Parent-Professional Collaboration in General and Special Education

Over the past decade, parent-school collaboration has become nationally recognized as a cornerstone in modern educational reforms. Every important program, including No Child Left Behind legislation, the Common Core State Standards, Response to Intervention, Race to the Top Awards, and many others, include and, in fact, require parent involvement.

Extensive research documents the consistent conclusion that family engagement and parent involvement are crucial to long-term outcomes for children (Miedel & Reynolds, 1999). A growing library of resources is now available to professionals and parents, fully accessible online and generally available free of charge.

One of the most prominent of these is the National Technical Assistance Centers, funded by the U.S. Department of Education, which provides information and resources to everyone involved in education, including teachers, parents, and students.

Another key resource for the consultant model discussed in this chapter, which can set the stage for building effective educational teams within the RTI process, is the National Dissemination Center for Children with Disabilities (http://nichcy.org/schools-administrators/recruiting/cop). Communities of

Figure 8.5 National Network of Partnership Schools Math Article: DIY Day: Dads Involved in Youth

DIY DAY: DADS INVOLVED IN YOUTH

Henry Timrod Elementary School
Florence, SC

"DIY" usually stands for Do It Yourself craft-making—but at Henry Timrod Elementary, when dads and other male relatives came to school with their children on a Saturday morning, it meant Dads Involved in Youth (DIY). Pre-K through sixth-grade students and their dads, uncles, grandfathers, and male community volunteers all worked together to construct their own birdfeeders and learn new math concepts along the way

One Saturday morning, 56 students and 48 male family members arrived at Henry Timrod and received a math skills sheet, clipboard, and pencil. The families ate a full breakfast, which was sponsored by a local church and restaurant.

After breakfast, everyone proceeded to the construction side of the cafeteria to obtain a birdhouse kit, tape measure, and screwdriver set, which was theirs to keep thanks to a grant from the Francis Marion University (FMU) Center of Excellence. Student-family teams received basic directions for building a birdfeeder and were shown a model. Then, working at long cafeteria tables, they started their projects. Eighteen volunteers—including male community leaders, FMU students, teachers' spouses, a local male artist, and a carpenter—walked around, assisting as needed.

Once students and their male relatives built their birdhouses, they worked together to complete related math activities. Teachers were on hand to help students recall concepts and skills in measurement, prediction, shape identification, and comparing angles.

Student-father groups took their wooden birdhouses to paint stations in the school breezeway. At the final measurement station, they measured birdseed donated by Lowe's and completed their math skills sheet. Students handed in a checklist of steps taken to make their birdhouses and their math skills sheet, showing over 80% mastery of math skills.

Each student-father team proudly carried home their birdhouse, birdseed, tape measure and screwdriver set, and a smile. For 29 fathers, uncles, and grandfathers, DIY Day was the first time they had attended a school event all year. One teacher commented, "Five of my students participated today. ...I'd only met the moms before. It was great to see and talk to their dads."

Community volunteers helped make DIY Day a success. One student, who did not have a male relative, partnered with a male volunteer mentor. The FMU grant covered costs and Lowe's suggested a more affordable project for next year, as well as other materials it could donate. The volunteer carpenter said, "Please make sure you invite me to this event again next year. I will have four more guys lined up ready to come help...I can't think of a better way to spend a Saturday morning."

Choosing a Saturday allowed male relatives to participate outside of the workweek, but transportation to school was difficult. FMU reported that the college may be able to help with transportation in the future. With more than 87% of Henry Timrod students eligible for free and reduced-price lunch, receiving breakfast on a Saturday was also viewed as a benefit.

At DIY Day, students learned math, constructed crafts, and built family-school partnerships. Most importantly, said one teacher, "Students were so proud to have their dads with them—that's a feeling in the atmosphere that's not even describable." Do it yourself crafting has never been so full of do-it-togetherness.

Type 4

MATH

Dawn Walker
Fifth-grade teacher
dawn.walker@fsd1.org

13

Source: http://www.csos.jhu.edu/p2000/ppp/2012/pdf/13.pdf. National Network of Partnership Schools (NNPS) at Johns Hopkins University, www.partnershipschools.org.

practice (CoPs) are described as "groups of people who share a concern or a passion for something they do and learn how to do it better as they interact regularly" (Wenger, 2006, para. 4). A CoP "is quite simply a group of people that agree to interact regularly to solve a persistent problem or improve practice in an area that is important to them" (IDEA Partnership, n.d.). In keeping with the values of a consultant relationship, all stakeholders are equally respected, not just as individuals, but for the special expertise that each brings to the discussion. Bill East, the executive director of the National Association of State Directors of Special Education and a former state director of special education, gave a strong endorsement of the consultant model of parent involvement, and a caution against the traditional client approach:

> I worked hard with stakeholders but I didn't work smart. More times than not, I didn't involve them up front in the decision making process. Thinking deeply about community building has led me to understand just how important it is to have stakeholder involvement from the very beginning (quoted in Cashman, Linehan, & Rosser, 2007, p. viii)

In the National Communities of Practice, parents are seen as experts in regard to their child's educational needs, involved in planning and decision making from the very beginning and throughout the educational process. Participants typically meet monthly via national or regional teleconference and discuss perspectives on educational issues that the members have selected as a critical problem or a significant opportunity for parent involvement.

The next section describes additional groups supporting parent involvement and promoting a consultant approach to parent-school collaboration in the process of assisting children to reach the benchmarks of the Common Core State Standards in mathematics. These include both general and special education orientation, remembering that federal and state mandates for inclusion have blurred the distinction between the two. In today's schools, every teacher is a special education teacher. In the same way, in almost every state, the standards and content of the Common Core apply equally to general and special education students.

Resources for Further Study

Parent Roadmaps to the Common Core State Standards— Mathematics

www.cgcs.org/Page/244

This website contains links to 10 documents outlining the Council of the Great City Schools' parent roadmaps in mathematics. These documents provide guidance to parents about what their children will be learning and how they can support that learning in Grades K–8. Three-year snapshots of each grade level showing how selected standards progress from year to year are provided for parents.

Wrightslaw

www.wrightslaw.com/advoc/articles/seven_steps.htm

Parents, educators, advocates, and attorneys go to this site for authoritative, reliable information about special and general education law and advocacy for students. This link accesses an article, "Seven Steps to Effective Parent Advocacy," which include ideas for planning and preparation for parent advocacy.

Common Core State Standards for Parents

www.ode.state.or.us/search/page/?id=3380

This site contains extensive resources for parents on the Common Core prepared by the Oregon Department of Education, some of which are presented in both English and Spanish. The website includes links to parent guides and toolkits as well as a searchable database of the standards in mathematics and English language arts.

U.S. Department of Education

www.ed.gov

The U.S. Department of Education's mission is to promote student achievement and preparation for global competitiveness by fostering educational excellence and ensuring equal access. Visit this site to access an extensive and authoritative collection of education-related information, including information on the Common Core State Standards and RTI best practices.

Families and Advocates Partnership for Education

www.fape.org

This site links families, advocates, and self-advocates to information about the Individuals with Disabilities Education Act. The project is designed to address the information needs of the six million families throughout the country whose children with disabilities receive special education services.

National Association of School Psychologists (NASP)

www.nasponline.org/publications/cq/39/6/idea-in-practice.aspx

The NASP website is a source of knowledge, resources, and information on the Common Core State Standards and RTI. It is the official organization for school psychologists, publishing materials relevant and available for all stakeholders. This link accesses an article by Mary Beth Klotz titled "Common Core State Standards: New Assessments to Replace Existing State Tests" and additional resources on the Common Core, assessments, and RTI.

K–8 California's Common Core State Standards Parent Handbook

www.empire.k12.ca.us/files/user/20/file/K-8%20California%27s %20Common%20Core%20Standards%20Parent%20Handbook%20 %28English%29.pdf

This parent guide was prepared by the California County Super-intendents Educational Services Association. It contains information for parents on the Common Core State Standards in mathematics and English language arts.

Education Resources and Information Center (ERIC)

www.eric.ed.gov

ERIC provides access to more than 1.3 million bibliographic records of journal articles and other education-related materials, with hundreds of new records added every week. Some of the references cited are available for download; others present abstracts and references to the journals of their original publication.

Iris Training Center

www.iris.peabody.vanderbilt.edu

The Iris Training Center offers free online interactive resources, including activities and case studies that translate research about the education of students with disabilities into practice. Their materials cover a wide variety of evidence-based topics, including behavior, RTI, learning strategies, and progress monitoring. This website also contains education briefs, a compendium of online resources from other sources on RTI (accessible by clicking on Resources).

National Center for Culturally Responsive Educational Systems

www.nccrest.org

This organization supports state education agencies and local school systems to ensure a quality, culturally responsive education for all students, including in the RTI process.

National Parent Teacher Association

www.pta.org/3816.htm

This website provides links to resources relating to family and school partnerships, including Common Core State Standards Initiative: Common Education Standards: What You Need to Know.

Handbook on Family and Community Engagement

www.schoolcommunitynetwork.org/downloads/FACEHandbook.pdf

This handbook by Sam Redding, Marilyn Murphy, and Pam Sheley was created with funding and support from the U.S. Department of Education's Office of Elementary and Secondary Education to the Academic Development Institute and the Center on Innovation & Improvement. This handbook provides educators, community leaders, and parents with a compendium of the best research and practice.

Parents' Guide to Student Success

http://pta.org/parents/content.cfm?ItemNumber=2583

The National PTA created guides for Grades K–8 and Grades 9–12 (one for English language arts/literacy and one for mathematics), which includes the following:

- key items that children should be learning in English language arts and mathematics in each grade, once the standards are fully implemented
- activities that parents can do at home to support their child's learning
- methods for helping parents build stronger relationships with their child's teacher
- tips for planning for college and career (high school only)

Common Core State Standards

www.corestandards.org

This website contains all the Common Core State Standards.

The Future of the
Common Core and RTI

Oh! what a revolution! and what a heart must I have, to contemplate without emotion that elevation and that fall! . . . They have found their punishment in their success. Laws overturned; tribunals subverted; industry without vigor; commerce expiring, the revenue unpaid, yet the people impoverished.

—Edmund Burke, *Reflections on
the Revolution in France* (1791/1955, p. 5)

Bliss was it in that dawn to be alive, but to be young was very heaven.

—William Wordsworth, *The Prelude* (1850/1970)

These completely opposing views on the French Revolution come from two of the most renowned English writers of the time. Wordsworth, toward the end of his life, recalled his joy as a young man in feeling himself part of a movement that would eventually eliminate despotism from Europe and open the door to democracy and freedom. Burke, writing in the midst of the same event, saw only the end of a traditional way of life. With two centuries of hindsight, it is easy to see that both were partly right, but neither caught the full scope of what was happening.

Massive changes in a nation or culture have a way of polarizing feeling, either for or against the movement. In American education, a philosophy of local control based on local standards has dominated the nation since the late nineteenth century. In 2014, a year from the publication of this book, the legislatures of forty-six states (as of early 2013) have declared that this paradigm will change radically, in what amounts to a revolution in education. Yong Zhao clearly described the revolutionary aspect of the changes ahead— and hinted at the tremendous difficulty we will face in untangling the threats from the benefits:

As American schools pour their resources into products, programs, and services to be Common Core ready in 2013, please keep in mind that the Common Core is a bet on the future of our children. While I have written about the Common Core many times before (e.g., Common Core vs. Common Sense, Common Core National Curriculum Standards), I wanted to ask all of us to ask again if the new world of education ushered in by the Common Core will be better than the old one scheduled to end in a year. (Zhao, 2013, p. 1)

Zhao points out that the Common Core was created by America's political and educational leaders because they saw our schools as fallen to a condition described as "chaotic, fragmented, unequal, obsolete, and failing" (p. 1)—the kinds of conditions that have led to revolutions of all types in recent history. But at the same time, he warns against zealotry in response to the great changes that lie ahead (the "bet on the future of our children"). If the most brilliant minds of the generation that lived through the French Revolution could not see the full implications of the events in front of them, it is probably good counsel not to become a full-throated advocate, either for or against the changes, particularly in the early stages.

The Common Core State Standards, RTI, and other revolutionary school reforms are fully underway, and the political momentum is not likely to be reversed. The time for determined opposition has passed. On the other hand, as with any new initiative, these reforms are still untested experiments with our children's future. There is little historical precedent, and only an anecdotal track record of success, that advocates can point to. The good or the harm that these programs do will depend entirely on the creativity, the sensitivity, the flexibility, the willingness to compromise and adapt, and the perseverance of the educators who put them into practice beginning in 2014.

This book is an attempt to offer a balanced picture of the complex interrelationships between the Common Core State Standards and Response to Intervention, without proselytizing them or suggesting a guarantee that either or both together can lead our schools to a brighter future. These are innovative tools, with great potential for helping creative teachers to improve their work with children. But they will only be as successful as the talent and determination of tens of thousands of teachers across the nation who adapt them to their own classes and are alert enough to recognize the signs from their students when changes need to be made.

We look forward to continuing our work with teachers as they learn how to use CCSS and RTI to improve the success of their students. That success can never be guaranteed by a government mandate or an educational program. It will come only from teachers who care enough about their students to stop at nothing until every one of them has achieved their full potential.

References

Ahmed, A., Clark-Jeavons, A., & Oldknow, A. (2004). How can teaching aids improve the quality of mathematics education? *Educational Studies in Mathematics, 56,* 313–328.

Arcavi, A. (2003). The role of visual representations in the teaching and learning of mathematics. *Educational Studies in Mathematics, 52,* 215–241.

Aud, S., Hussar, W., Kena, G., Bianco, K., Frohlich, L., Kemp, J., & Tahan, K. (2011). *The condition of education 2011* (NCES 2011–033). Washington, DC: U.S. Government Printing Office. Retrieved from http://nces.ed.gov/pubs2011/2011033.pdf

Baker, S., Gersten, R., & Lee, D. (2002). A synthesis of empirical research on teaching mathematics to low-achieving students. *Elementary School Journal, 103,* 51–73.

Barker, J. A. (2001). *Joel Barker's the new business of paradigms: 21st century edition.* Retrieved from http://www.thenewbusinessofparadigms.com/media/preview/Transcript21stCentPreview_NBOP.pdf

Barrera, M., Liu, K., Thurlow, M., Shyyan, V., Yan, M., & Chamberlain, S. (2006). *Math strategy instruction for students with disabilities who are learning English* (ELLs with Disabilities Report 16). Minneapolis: University of Minnesota, National Center on Educational Outcomes. Retrieved from http://education.umn.edu/NCEO/OnlinePubs/ELLsDis16

Bateman, D., & Bateman, C. F. (2001). *A principal's guide to special education.* Arlington, VA: Council for Exceptional Children.

Beggs, J. J. (1995). The institutional environment: Implications for race and gender inequality in the U.S. labor market. *American Sociological Review, 60,* 612–633.

Brown, C. L., Cady, J. A., & Taylor, P. M. (2009). Problem solving and the English language learner. *Mathematics Teaching in the Middle Schools, 14,* 532–539.

Bryant, D. P., Bryant, B. R., Gersten, R., Scammacca, N., & Chavetz, M. M. (2008). Mathematics intervention for first- and second-grade students with mathematical difficulties: The effects of Tier 2 intervention delivered as booster lessons. *EBSCO: Remedial and Special Education, 29*(1), 20–32. Retrieved from http://rse.sagepub.com/content/29/1/20.full.pdf+html

Bryant, D. P., Bryant, B. R., Gersten, R. M., Scammacca, N. N., Funk, C., Winter, A., . . . Pool, C. (2008). The effects of Tier 2 intervention on the mathematics performance of first-grade students who are at risk for mathematics difficulties. *Learning Disabilities Quarterly, 31*(1), 47–63.

Buffum, A., Mattos, M., & Weber, C. (2010). The why behind RTI. *Educational Leadership*, 68(2), 10–16.

Burke, E. (1955). *Reflections on the Revolution in France.* Chicago, IL: H. Regnery. (Original work published 1791)

Burton, D., & Kappenberg, J. (2012). *The complete guide to RTI: An implementation toolkit.* Thousand Oaks, CA: Corwin.

Capps, L. R., & Pickreign, J. (1993). Language connections in mathematics: A critical part of mathematics instruction. *Arithmetic Teacher, 41*(1), 8–12.

Carr, E., Levin, L., McConnachie, G., Carlson, J., Kemp, D., & Smith, C. (1994). *Communication-based intervention for problem behavior: A user's guide for producing positive change.* Baltimore, MD: Paul H. Brookes.

Carr, J. F., & Harris D. E. (2001). *Succeeding with standards linking curriculum, assessment, and action planning.* Alexandria, VA: Association for Supervision and Curriculum Development.

Case, L., Harris, K., & Graham, S. (1992). Improving the mathematical problem-solving skills of students with learning disabilities: Self-regulated strategy development. *Journal of Special Education, 26*(1), 1–19.

Cashman, J., Linehan, P., & Rosser, M. (2007). *Communities of practice: A new approach to solving complex educational problems.* Alexandria, VA: National Association of State Directors of Special Education.

CAST. (1999–2012). *UDL questions and answers.* Retrieved from http://www.cast.org/udl/faq/index.html#q3

Clark, J. P. (1998). Functional behavioral assessment and behavioral intervention plans: Implementing the student discipline provisions of IDEA '97. *Section Connection, 4*(2), 6–7.

Clark, J. P., & Tilly, W. D. (2010). The evolution of response to intervention. In J. P. Clark & M. E. Alvarez (Eds.), *Response to intervention: A guide for school social workers* (pp. 3–20). New York, NY: Oxford University Press.

Clark, K. B., & Clark, M. P. (1950). Emotional factors in racial identification and preference in negro children. *Journal of Negro Education, 19,* 341–350.

Common Core State Standards Initiative. (2012). *Key points in mathematics.* Retrieved from http://www.corestandards.org/about-the-standards/key-points-in-mathematics

Connor, D. J., & Ferri, B. A. (2007). The conflict within: Resistance to inclusion and other paradoxes in special inclusion. *Disability and Society, 22*(1), 63–77.

Council of Chief State School Officers. (2010). *Common Core Standards for mathematics.* Washington, DC: National Governors Association, Center for Best Practices, Council of Chief State School Officers.

Covey, S. (1989). *The seven habits of highly effective people.* New York, NY: Free Press.

Cummins, J. (2000) *Language, power and pedagogy: Bilingual children in the crossfire.* Clevedon, UK: Multilingual Matters.

Cummins, J. (2005). Teaching the language of academic success: A framework for school based language policies. In California State Department of Education, *Schooling and language minority students: A theoretic practical framework* (3rd ed., pp. 3–32). Los Angeles: California State University, Los Angeles, Evaluation, Dissemination and Assessment Center.

Deno, S. L. (2003). Curriculum-based measures: Development and perspectives. *Assessment for Effective Intervention, 28*, 3–12.

Dodd, A. W., & Konzal, J. L. (2000). Parents and educators as partners: Conducting students learning. *High School Magazine, 7*(5), 8–13.

Dove, M. G., & Honigsfeld, A. (2013). *Common Core for the not-so-common learner, Grades K–5: English language arts strategies.* Thousand Oaks, CA: Corwin.

Echevarria, J., Vogt, M. E., & Short, D. (2012). *Making content comprehensible for English language learners: The SIOP model* (4th ed.). Boston, MA: Allyn & Bacon.

Eeds, M., & Cockrum, W. A. (1985). Teaching word meanings by expanding schemata vs. dictionary work vs. reading in context. *Journal of Reading, 28*, 492–497.

EngageNY. (2012). *Pedagogical shifts demanded by the Common Core State Standards.* Retrieved from http://www.engageny.org/sites/default/files/resource/attach ments/common-core-shifts.pdf

Ensign, J. (1997). *Linking life's experiences to classroom math.* Paper presented at the Annual Meeting of the American Educational Research Association, Chicago, IL. (ERIC Document Reproduction Service No. ED412093)

Ernst-Slavit, G., & Slavit, D. (2007). Educational reform, mathematics, and diverse learners: Meeting the needs of all students. *Multicultural Education, 14*(4), 20–27.

Esparza Brown, J., & Doolittle, J. (2008). *A cultural, linguistic, and ecological framework for Response to Intervention with English language learners.* Tempe, AZ: NCCREST. Retrieved from http://www.nccrest.org/Briefs/Framework_for_RTI.pdf

Fathman, A. K., Quinn, M. E., & Kessler, C. (1992). *Teaching science to English learners, grades 4-8.* Washington, DC: U.S. Department of Education, Office of Bilingual Education and Minority Languages Affairs.

Fisher, D., & Frey, N. (2010). *Enhancing RTI: How to ensure success with effective classroom instruction and intervention.* Alexandria, VA: Association for Supervision and Curriculum Development.

Flores, S. M., Batalova, J., & Fix, M. (2012). *The educational trajectories of English language learners in Texas.* Washington, DC: Migration Policy Institute.

Foegen, A. (2008). Algebra progress monitoring and interventions for students with learning disabilities. *Learning Disability Quarterly, 31*, 65–78.

Frayer, D., Frederick, W. C., & Klausmeier, H. J. (1969). *A schema for testing the level of cognitive mastery.* Madison: Wisconsin Center for Education Research.

Friend, M., & Cook, L. (1995). Co-teaching: Guidelines for creating effective practices. *Focus on Exceptional Children, 28*(3), 1–16.

Friend, M., & Hurley-Chamberlain, D. (2008). *Is co-teaching effective?* Retrieved from http://oldsite.cec.sped.org/AM/Template.cfm?Section=Support_for_ Teachers&template=/CM/ContentDisplay.cfm&ContentID=7504

Fuchs, D., & Fuchs, L. S. (2005). Responsiveness-to-intervention: A blueprint for practitioners, policymakers, and parents. *Teaching Exceptional Children, 38*(1), 57–61.

Fuchs, D., & Fuchs, L. S. (2006). Introduction to responsiveness-to-intervention: What, why, and how valid is it? *Reading Research Quarterly, 4*, 93–99.

Fuchs, L., Fuchs, D., Compton, D., Bryant, J., Hamlett, C., & Seethaler, P. (2007). Mathematics screening and progress monitoring at first grade: Implications for responsiveness to intervention. *Exceptional Children, 73*, 311–330.

Gersten, R., Beckmann, S., Clarke, B., Foegen, A., Marsh, L., Star, J. R., & Witzel, B. (2009). *Assisting students struggling with mathematics: Response to Intervention (RTI) for elementary and middle schools* (NCEE 2009–4060). Washington, DC: National Center for Education Evaluation and Regional Assistance, Institute of Education Sciences U.S. Department of Education. Retrieved from http://ies.ed.gov/ncee/wwc/publications/practiceguides

Gersten, R., Chard, D. J., Jayanthi, M., Baker, S. K., Morphy, P., & Flojo, J. (2009). Mathematics instruction for students with learning disabilities: A meta-analysis of instructional components. *Review of Educational Research, 79*, 1202–1242.

Gersten, R., & Clarke, B. S. (2007). *Effective strategies for teaching students with difficulties in mathematics.* Retrieved from http://www.nctm.org/news/content.aspx?id=8452

Gersten, R., Clarke, B., Haymond, K., & Jordan, N. (2011). *Screening for mathematics difficulties in K–3 students* (2nd ed.). Portsmouth, NH: RMC Research Corporation, Center on Instruction.

Greenberg, D. (1998). *Comic strip math: 40 reproducible cartoons with dozens of funny story problems that build essential skills.* New York, NY: Scholastic.

Greenwood, S. C., & Flanigan, K. (2007). Overlapping vocabulary and comprehension: Context clues compliment semantic gradients, *Reading Teacher, 61*, 249–254.

Griffith, K. G., Cooper, M. J., & Ringlaben, R. P. (2002). A three dimensional model for the inclusion of children with disabilities. *Electronic Journal for Inclusive Education, 1*(6). Retrieved from http://corescholar.libraries.wright.edu/ejie

Grossman, T., Reyna, R., & Shipto, S. (2011). *Realizing the potential: How governors can lead effective implementation of the Common Core State Standards.* Washington, DC: National Governors Association.

Grouws, D., & Cebulla, K. (2000). *Improving student achievement in mathematics.* Geneva, Switzerland: International Academy of Education, International Bureau of Education.

Hang, Q., & Rabren, K. (2009). An examination of co-teaching: Perspectives and efficacy indicators. *Remedial and Special Education, 30*, 259–268.

Hitchcock, C., Meyer, A., Rose, D., & Jackson, R. (2002). Providing new access to the general curriculum: Universal design for learning. *Teaching Exceptional Children, 35*(2), 8–17.

Hosp, M., Hosp, J., & Howell, K. (2007). *The ABCs of CBM: A practical guide to curriculum-based measurement.* New York, NY: Guilford Press.

Hutton, J. B., Dubes, R., & Muir, S. (1992). Estimating trends in progress monitoring data: A comparison of simple line-fitting methods. *School Psychology Review, 21*, 300–312.

IDEA Partnership. (n.d.). *Creating community.* Retrieved from http://ideapartnership.org/creating-community.html

Iowa Department of Education, Bureau of Children, Families, and Community Services. (2006). *Progress monitoring for teachers of students who have visual disabilities.* Des Moines, IA: Author. Retrieved from http://www.iowa.gov/edu cate/index.php?option=com_docman&task=doc_download&gid=3313

Irvin, J. L. (1990). *Vocabulary knowledge: Guidelines for instruction.* Washington, DC: National Education Association.

Kahneman, D. (2011). *Thinking, fast and slow.* New York. NY: Farrar, Straus and Giroux.

Kamii, C., & Russell, K. (2012). Elapsed time: Why is it so difficult to teach? *Journal for Research in Mathematics Education, 43,* 296–315.

Karagiannis, A., Stainback, S., & Stainback, W. (1996). Historical overview of inclusion. In S. Stainback & W. Stainback (Eds.), *Inclusion: A guide for educators* (pp. 17–28). Baltimore, MD: Brookes.

Katz, L. (1989). *Pedagogical issues in early childhood education.* (ERIC Document Reproduction Service No. ED321840)

Kendall, J. (2011). *Understanding Common Core State Standards.* Alexandria, VA: Association for Supervision and Curriculum Development.

Kester Phillips, D. C., Bardsley, M. E., Bach, T., & GibbsBrown, K. (2009). "But I teach math!" The journey of middle school mathematics teachers and literacy coaches learning to integrate literacy strategies into the math instruction. *Education, 129.* 467–472.

Khan, Y. (2012). *Special education reform brings city more in line with national trend.* Retrieved from http://www.schoolbook.org/2012/08/09/special-ed-reform-brings-city-more-in-line-with-national-trend

Kilpatrick, J., Swafford, J., & Findell, B. (Eds.). (2001). *Adding it up: Helping children learn mathematics.* Washington, DC: National Academy Press.

Kloo, A., & Zigmond, N. (2008). Co-teaching revisited: Redrawing the blueprint. *Preventing School Failure, 52*(2), 12–20.

Kroesbergen, E. H., & Van Luit, J. E. H. (2003). Mathematics interventions for children with special educational needs: A meta-analysis. *Remedial and Special Education, 24,* 97–115.

Krugman, P. (2003, November 13). The one-handed economist. *The Economist,* pp. 11–13. Retrieved from http://www.economist.com

Lehrer, J. (2007). *Proust was a neuroscientist.* Boston, MA: Houghton Mifflin.

Lent, R. W., Brown, S. D., & Hackett, G. (2000). Contextual supports and barriers to career choice: A social cognitive analysis. *Journal of Counseling Psychology, 47,* 36–49.

Lewis, J. (1996). *Perspective of parent involvement in public education.* http://www .amschool.edu.sv/easite/parent_education.aspx?mnu_id=6&slc=143

Maker, C. (1977). *Providing programs for the gifted handicapped.* Reston, VA: Council for Exceptional Children.

Marzano, R. J. (2004). *Building background knowledge for academic achievement.* Alexandria, VA: Association for Supervision and Curriculum Development.

Marzano, R. J., & Pickering, D. J. (2005). *Building academic vocabulary,* Alexandria, VA: Association for Supervision and Curriculum Development.

Maryland State Department of Education. (1997–2013). *Using the state curriculum: Mathematics, grade K.* Retrieved from http://mdk12.org/instruction/prereqs/ mathematics/gradeK/1A2b.html

Marzano, R. J., & Simms, J. (2013). *Vocabulary for the common core*. Bloomington, IN: Marzano Research Laboratory.

Maslow, A. H. (1943). A theory of human motivation. *Psychological Review, 50*, 370–396.

McKellar, D. (2007). *Math doesn't suck: How to survive middle school math*. New York, NY: Penguin.

Meador, D. (2013). *Tips for parents: School tips for parents from a principal*. Retrieved from http://teaching.about.com/od/ParentalInvolvement/a/Tips-For-Parents .htm

Mellard, D., & Johnson, E. (2008). *RTI: A practitioner's guide to implementing response to intervention*. Thousand Oaks, CA: Corwin.

Miedel, W. T., & Reynolds, A. J. (1999). Parent involvement in early intervention for disadvantaged children: Does it matter? *Journal of School Psychology, 37*, 379–402.

Miller, D. L. (1993). Making the connection with language. *Arithmetic Teacher, 40*, 311–316.

Mitchell, C. (2008). *Parent involvement in public education: A literature review*. Philadelphia, PA: Research for Action.

Morgan, P. L. (2009). *Parenting an adult with disabilities or special needs*. New York, NY: AMACOM Books.

Mrs. Glosser's Math Goodies. (1998–2013). *Math goodies*. Retrieved from http://www.mathgoodies.com

Muller, E., Friend, M., & Hurley-Chamberlain, D. A. (2009, May). State-level approaches to co-teaching. *inForum*, pp. 1–7. Retrieved from http://projectforum .org/docs/state-levelapproachestoco-teaching.pdf

Mullis, I. V. S., Martin, M. O., Foy, P., & Arora, A. (2012). *TIMSS 2011 international results in mathematics*. Chestnut Hill, MA: Boston College, TIMSS & PIRLS International Study Center.

Murawski, W. (2008). Five keys to co-teaching in inclusive classrooms. *The School Administrator, 65*(8). Retrieved from http://www.aasa.org/SchoolAdministrator .aspx

National Association of State Directors of Special Education. (2005). *Response to intervention: Policy considerations and implementation*. Alexandria, VA: Author.

National Center on Student Progress Monitoring. (n.d.). *What is progress monitoring?* Retrieved from http://www.studentprogress.org

National Council of Teachers of English. (2008). *English language learners. A policy research brief*. Retrieved from http://www.ncte.org/library/NCTEFiles/Resources/ PolicyResearch/ELLResearchBrief.pdf

National Council of Teachers of Mathematics. (1989). *Curriculum and evaluation standards for school mathematics*. Reston, VA: Author.

National Council of Teachers of Mathematics. (2000). *Principles and standards for school mathematics*. Reston, VA: Author.

National Council of Teachers of Mathematics. (2008a). *English language learners*. Retrieved from http://www.ncte.org/library/NCTEFiles/Resources/PolicyRese arch/ELLResearchBrief.pdf

National Council of Teachers of Mathematics. (2008b). *Teaching mathematics to English language learners*. Retrieved from http://www.nctm.org/about/content .aspx?id=16135

National Governors Association Center for Best Practices, Council of Chief State School Officers. (2010). *Common Core state mathematics standards*. Washington, DC: National Governors Association. Retrieved from http://www.nga.org/cms/center

National Institute of Mental Health. (2013). *Autism spectrum disorders (pervasive developmental disorders)*. Retrieved from http://www.nimh.nih.gov/health/topics/autism-spectrum-disorders-pervasive-developmental-disorders/index.shtml

National Mathematics Advisory Panel. (2008). *Foundations for success: The final report of the national mathematics advisory panel*. Washington, DC: U.S. Department of Education.

Neuschwander, C. (1999). *Sir cumference and the dragon of pi*. Watertown, MA: Charlesbridge.

New York State Education Department. (2012). *New York State P–12 common core learning standards for mathematics*. Retrieved from http://www.engageny.org/sites/default/files/resource/attachments/nysp12cclsmath.pdf

North Carolina Department of Public Instruction. (2012). *6th grade mathematics: Unpacked contents*. Retrieved from http://www.dpi.state.nc.us/docs/acre/standards/common-core-tools/unpacking/math/6th.pdf

North Carolina State University, Center for Universal Design. (1997). *The principles of universal design*. Retrieved from http://www.ncsu.edu/www/ncsu/design/sod5/cud/about_ud/udprinciplestext.htm

Pierce, M., & Fontaine, L. (2009). Designing vocabulary instruction in mathematics. *The Reading Teacher, 63*, 239–243.

Reeves, D. B. (2010). *Transforming professional development into student results*. Alexandria, VA: Association for Supervision and Curriculum Development.

Richardson, S., & Wilkinson, M. E. (2005). Challenges of instructing secondary English language learner students in mathematics: Survey of Texas teachers. *Psychology of Mathematics and Education, 12*, 1–2.

Roberts, S. O. (2012). *The relationship between parent involvement and mathematics achievement in struggling mathematics learners*. Retrieved from http://steinhardt.nyu.edu/opus/issues/2011/spring/involvement_and_math

Rose, D., & Meyer, A. (2000). Universal design for learning. *Journal of Special Education Technology, 15*(1), 67–70.

Rose, D. H., & Meyer, A. (2002). *Teaching every student in the digital age: Universal design for learning*. Alexandra, VA: Association for Supervision and Curriculum Development.

Rose, L. C., Gallup, A. M., & Elam, S. M. (1997). The 29th annual Phi Delta Kappa/Gallup poll of the public's attitudes toward the public schools. *Phi Delta Kappan, 79*(1), 41–56.

Rosenshine, B. (2012). Principles of instruction: Research-based strategies that all teachers should know. *American Educator*. Retrieved from http://www.aft.org/pdfs/americaneducator/spring2012/Rosenshine.pdf

Ross, S. H. (1989). Parts, wholes, and place value: A developmental view. *Arithmetic Teacher, 36*, 47–51.

RTI Action Network. (n.d.). *What is RTI?* Retrieved from http://www.rtinetwork.org/learn/what/whatisrti

Rubenstein, R. N. (n.d.). *Mathematical symbolization: Challenges across levels.* Retrieved from http://tsg.icme11.org/document/get/853

Schell, V. J. (1982). Learning partners: Reading and mathematics. *Reading Teacher, 35,* 544–548.

Schielack, J., Charles, R., Clements, S., Duckett, P., Fennell, F., Lewandowski, S., . . . Zbeik, R. M. (2006). *Curriculum focal points for prekindergarten through grade 8 mathematics: A quest for coherence. Reston, VA:* National Council of Teachers of Mathematics.

Schneider, C. (2009). Equal is not enough: Current issues in inclusive education in the eyes of children. *Institutional Journal of Education, 1*(1), 1–14.

Scott, S. S., McGuire, J. M., & Shaw, S. F. (2003). Universal design for instruction: A new paradigm for teaching adults in postsecondary education. *Remedial and Special Education, 24,* 369–379.

Scruggs, T., Mastropieri, M., & McDuffie, K. (2007). Co-teaching in inclusive classrooms: A meta-synthesis of qualitative research. *Exceptional Children, 73,* 392–416.

Scull, A. (2012, January 6). Rules of thumb. *London Times Literary Supplement,* pp. 5–7.

Short, D., & Echevarria, J. (2004/2005). Promoting academic literacy for English language learners. *Educational Leadership, 62*(4), 8–13.

Shymansky, J., Marberry, C., & Jorgensen, M. (1977). Science and mathematics are spoken and written here: Promoting science and mathematics literacy in the classroom. In D. Holdzkom & P. B. Lut (Eds.), *Reform in math and science education: Issues for the classroom* (CD-ROM). Columbus, OH: Eisenhower National Clearinghouse.

Simon, C. A. (2013). *Using the think-pair-share technique.* Retrieved from http://www.readwritethink.org/professional-development/strategy-guides/using-think-pair-share-30626.html

Slavit, D., & Ernst-Slavit, G. (2007). Teaching mathematics and English to English language learners simultaneously. *Middle School Journal, 39*(2), 4–11.

Sloutsky, V. M., & Yarlas, A. S. (2000). Problem representation I novices and experts: Part 2. Underlying processing mechanisms. In L. R. Gleitman & A. K. Joshi (Eds.), *Proceedings of the 22nd Annual Conference of the Cognitive Science Society* (pp. 475–480). Mahwah, NJ: Lawrence Erlbaum.

Snyder, T. D., & Dillow, S. A. (2012). *Digest of education statistics 2011.* Washington, DC: U.S. Department of Education, National Center for Education Statistics.

Sousa, D. A. (2006). *How the brain learns.* Thousand Oaks, CA: Corwin.

Tallis, R. (2011). *Aping mankind: Neuromania, Darwinists and the misrepresentation of humanity.* Durham, UK: Acumen.

Tiegerman-Farber, E., & Radziewicz, C. (1997). *Collaborative decision making: The pathway to inclusion.* New York, NY: Prentice Hall.

Tilly, W. D., III. (2002). School psychology as a problem solving enterprise. In A. Thomas & J. Grimes (Eds.), *Best practices in school psychology IV* (pp. 21–36). Bethesda, MD: National Association of School Psychologists.

U.S. Census Bureau. (2012). *Most children younger than age 1 are minorities, Census Bureau reports.* Retrieved from http://www.census.gov/newsroom/releases/archives/population/cb12-90.html

U.S. Department of Education. (2003). *Mathematics and science initiative concept paper*. Retrieved from http://www.ed.gov/rschstat/research/progs/mathscience/concept_paper.pdf

U.S. Department of Education. (n.d.). *Building the legacy: IDEA 2004*. Retrieved from http://idea.ed.gov

U.S. National Commission on Excellence in Education. (1983). *A nation at risk: The imperative for educational reform*. Washington, DC: U.S. Department of Education. Retrieved from http://www2.ed.gov/pubs/EdReformStudies/EdReforms/chap1d.html

Vygotsky, L. S. (1978). *Mind in society: The development of higher psychological processes* (M. Cole, V. John-Steiner, S. Scribner, & E. Sauberman, Eds. and Trans.). Cambridge, MA: Harvard University Press. (Original work published 1934)

Wenger, E. (2006). *Communities of practice: A brief introduction*. Retrieved from http://www.ewenger.com/theory/index.htm

Wiggins, G., & McTighe, J. (2005). *Understanding by design*. Alexandria, VA: Association for Supervision and Curriculum Development.

Wordsworth, W. (1970). *The prelude*. New York, NY: Oxford University Press. (Original work published 1850)

Wright, J. (2007). *RTI toolkit: A practical guide for schools*. Port Chester, NY: Dude.

Zhao, Y. (2013). Five key questions about the Common Core Standards. *The Washington Post*. Retrieved from http://www.washingtonpost.com/blogs/answer-sheet/wp/2013/01/08/five-key-questions-about-the-common-core-standards

Zubal-Ruggieri, R., & Smith, V. (Eds.). (2003). *Inclusion in education: Issues and resources*. Syracuse, NY: Syracuse University, National Resource Center on Supported Living and Choice Center on Human Policy.

Index

CORWIN

A SAGE Company

The Corwin logo—a raven striding across an open book—represents the union of courage and learning. Corwin is committed to improving education for all learners by publishing books and other professional development resources for those serving the field of PreK–12 education. By providing practical, hands-on materials, Corwin continues to carry out the promise of its motto: **"Helping Educators Do Their Work Better."**